Michael DiGiacomo, MBA

Published in New York, USA
November 2014

First Edition Published 2011

PLEASE DO NOT MAKE ILLEGAL COPIES OF THIS BOOK
COPYRIGHT © 2014 MICHAEL DIGIACOMO
ALL RIGHTS RESERVED

Any redistribution or reproduction of part or all of the contents in any form is prohibited. You may not, except with my express written permission, distribute or commercially exploit the content. Nor may you transmit it or store it on any other website or other form of electronic retrieval system.

ISBN: 978-0-9915079-5-5

A Message From Michael

Thank you for your interest in 109 Phrasal Verbs.

My name is Michael DiGiacomo, and I am a native New Yorker. I have been helping language students learn English since the early 1990's. I began my formal language-teaching career in Sendai, Japan in 1994. Since then, I have worked in the ESL field as an instructor, a teacher trainer, an academic director, and a language school director. In 2004, I earned an MBA in Global Management. Now, I am the owner of Happy English, an English tutoring company in New York City. I teach students from all over the world here in New York, and online in their country.

I believe that language study should be both enjoyable and practical. In 2010 I started a website to provide a variety of English lessons to students all over the world. I set out to create lessons that were practical, easy to understand, and useful for self-study. In June of 2014, I started the Happy English Podcast to provide portable audio lessons for convenient English Study. Many of my students have given me inspiration for these lessons and this book grew out of some of those ideas.

You can find my website at **www.myhappyenglish.com**
Phrasal verbs are commonly used in everyday, conversational English. I encourage you to study the lessons in this book, and begin using these phrasal verbs in your conversations. You will sound more natural when you do so.

Changes in Volume II:
- 109 +11 Bonus Phrasal Verbs
- 720 Examples Sentences
- 12 Quizzes
- 12 Practice Exercises
- 10 Bonus Vocabulary Lessons
- 5 Survival English Lessons

As always, thanks for studying with me.

Table of Contents

A Message From Michael 2
Table of Contents 3
Key Points About Phrasal Verbs 10
1: back away 11
2: back up (1) 12
3: back up (2) 13
4: block off 14
5: bounce off 15
6: break down (1) 16
7: break down (2) 17
8: break in 18
9: break into (1) 19
10: break into (2) 20
Quiz 1 21
Practice Section 1 23
Confusing Words 1: Appointment, Reservation, Plans 24
11: break out (of) 25
12: break up (with) 26
13: bring down 27
14: bring up (1) 28
15: bring up (2) 29
16: butt in / into 30
17: call back 31
18: call off 32
19: call on 33
20: call up 34

3

Quiz 2 ....**35**
Practice Section 2 ....**37**
Confusing Words 2: Borrow vs. Lend..**38**
21: calm down..**39**
22: cheer up **40**
23: clam up...**41**
24: clean up..**42**
25: clear up **43**
26: count on **44**
27: cut down (on) **45**
28: cut out **46**
29: drag on..**47**
30: dress up **48**
Quiz 3..**49**
Practice Section 3 ....**51**
Confusing Words 3: During vs. While **52**
31: drop by..**53**
32: drop off **54**
33: eat out **55**
34: fall through..**56**
35: figure out..**57**
36: fill in..**58**
37: fill out **59**
38: fill up...**60**
39: find out..**61**
40: flip out (over) **62**
Quiz 4..**63**

Practice Section 4 65
Confusing Words 4: Taste and Flavor 66
41: freak out 67
42: get away (from) 68
43: get into 69
44: get out of 70
45: give away 71
46: give in/into 72
47: give up 73
48: go over 74
49: go under 75
50: grow up 76
Quiz 5 77
Practice Section 5 79
Confusing Words 5: Cost, Spend, & Take 80
51: hang around / out 81
52: hang on (to) 82
53: hold back 83
54: hold on (for) 84
55: hold on to 85
56: hook up (with) 86
57: keep on 87
58: kick back (at) 88
59: kick off 89
60: look down on 90
Quiz 6 91
Practice Section 6 93

Confusing Words 6: Fun and Funny 94
61: look for 95
62: look forward to 96
63: look into 97
64: look like 98
65: look out for 99
66: look over 100
67: look up to 101
68: luck out 102
69: make up (with) 103
70: mix up 104
Quiz 7 105
Practice Section 7 107
Confusing Words 7 Hard vs. Hardly 108
71: mull over 109
72: pick out 110
73: pick up 111
74: pop up 112
75: put away (1) 113
76: put away (2) 114
77: put down 115
78: put off 116
79: put on 117
80: put out (1) 118
Quiz 8 119
Practice Section 8 121
Confusing Words 8 Hope and Wish 122

81: put out (2) 123
82: put together 124
83: put up 125
84: put up with 126
85: ramp up 127
86: rule out 128
87: run away (from) 129
88: run into (1) 130
89: run into (2) 131
90: run out of 132
Quiz 9 133
Practice Section 9 135
Confusing Words 9 Meet Vs. See 136
91: run over (1) 137
92: run over (2) 138
93: show up 139
94: sleep in 140
95: sort out 141
96: stick to 142
97: take after 143
98: take apart 144
99: take back (1) 145
100: take back (2) 146
Quiz 10 147
Practice Section 10 149
Confusing Words 10 By Vs. Until 150
101: take off (1) 151

7

102: take off (2) 152
103: take out (of) 153
104: tell off 154
105: think over 155
106: think up 156
107: throw away 157
108: try on 158
109: turn away 159
110: turn back 160
Quiz 11 161
Practice Section 11 163
111: turn down (1) 164
112: turn down (2) 165
113: turn off 166
114: turn on 167
115: turn out 168
116: turn up (1) 169
117: turn up (2) 170
118: use up 171
119: wipe off 172
120: work out 173
Quiz 12 174
Practice Section 12 176
Quiz Answer Key 177
Survival English Tip 1 – The Tip System in America 178
Survival English Tip 2 – Regular Greetings 180
Survival English Tip 3 – Five Key Words To Order Food 182

Survival English Tip 4 – American Culture 184

Survival English Tip 5 – Doctors, hospitals, clinics 186

Other paperbacks & eBooks by Michael DiGiacomo........ 188

Key Points About Phrasal Verbs

1. A **phrasal verb** is a combination of a verb & a preposition used as an idiom, like "put out." **Put** is the verb, and **out** is the preposition.

2. In everyday English, especially conversational English, we prefer using **phrasal verbs**. Both of the following sentences are correct, but the first one is more commonly used:
   - Please **put out** your cigarette.
   - Please **extinguish** your cigarette.

3. We can separate some **phrasal verbs** and put the *direct object* between the verb and the preposition, or after the preposition"
   - Please **turn on** *the lights*.
   - Please **turn** *the lights* **on**.

4. In cases like 4 above, if you use a pronoun, it must come between the verb and the preposition. A pronoun never follows the preposition in a **phrasal verb,** if the **phrasal verb** can be separated:
   - I **turned** it **on**. *Not, I turned on it*

5. Some **phrasal verbs** are not separable and the *direct object* comes after the position:
   - I **called on** *Steve* when I was in Miami.

6. Some **phrasal verbs** have a fixed position. This means that the *direct object* comes between the verb and the preposition:
   - We **bounced** *our* **idea** off the boss.

1: back away

Meaning
- To retreat; to withdraw; to step back; to move away.

Usage
- A person can **back away** or **back away from** something.

Not Separable
- **back away**

Examples
- I **backed away** when I saw my angry boss walk into the office.

- Joe **backed away** from a fight.

- Everyone **backed away** from the suspicious package on the train.

- The union **backed away** from their demand for more vacation time.

- The executive group **backed away** from their original idea to expand the operation to Europe.

- The computer company said it wouldn't **back away** from its plan to outsource production to Cambodia.

2: back up (1)

Meaning:
- To walk, move, drive, or go in a backward direction.

Usage:
- People can **back up** (themselves), or **back up** objects like cars, machines, and furniture.

Separable:
- **back up**
- **back up** something
- **back** something **up**

Examples:
- I almost hit the lamp post when I **backed up** my car.
- Can you **back** that desk **up** a little bit?
- When we **backed up** the copy machine, we dropped it on Jack's foot.
- The truck **backed up** into the loading dock to pick up the cargo.
- Can you **back up** a little bit? I want to get everyone in the photo.
- If I **back** this desk **up** any more, I won't be able to sit behind it.

We also use **back up** in the computer and technology world. As a verb, **back up** means to save a copy of a file. As a noun, **back up** means the saved file

- I **backed up** my vacation photos.
- We **back up** the server once a day.
- I have a **back up** of that file.
- Please save a **back up** of your work.

12

3: back up (2)

Meaning
- To support a person, business, project, etc. To subsidize; to encourage.

Usage
- Someone can **back up** a person emotionally or something financially, such as parents can **back up** their children with money and/or encouragement.

Separable
- **back up** something/someone
- **back** something/someone **up**

Examples
- The business owner **backed up** the company's expansion with his own funds.

- I **backed** Tom **up** for a little while when he lost his job.

- My parents **backed** me **up** when I had trouble in college.

- John's family **backed up** his new business with a loan.

- Jack **backed** me **up** when I went to the boss's office to complain about working overtime.

- I told Joe that I would **back** him **up** at the meeting.

4: block off

Meaning
- To obstruct the passage of something; to barricade; to inhibit.

Usage
- Someone or something can **block off** a road, path, etc. An object, like a tree, or a person, like a police officer can block off a street.

Separable
- **block off** something/someone
- **block** something/someone **off**

Examples
- I couldn't see the CEO when he gave his speech because several tall people **blocked off** my view.

- Everybody was wondering why Jack **blocked off** his view of Jane with his computer monitor, but later we found out she rejected his invitation for a date.

- The board of directors tried to **block off** the acquisition of the company by their main rival, but they failed.

- The police **blocked off** the entrance to the train station during the blackout.

- After the storm, a fallen tree **blocked off** the sidewalk.

- The fire engine **blocked** the road **off** for several hours.

5: bounce off

Meaning
- To discuss something with someone in order to get their opinion of it.

Usage
- A person **bounces** something **off** someone. You can **bounce** an idea or plan **off** someone.

Fixed
- **bounce** something **off** someone

Examples
- I **bounced** my new marketing idea **off** my boss.

- Jack said he wanted to **bounce** something **off** me, so I am meeting him for lunch.

- Can I **bounce** something **off** you?

- Why don't we **bounce** this idea **off** the manager before trying it.

- Bob **bounced** some ideas **off** his wife about where to go on vacation.

- You should **bounce** that project idea **off** the teacher before you start working on it.

6: break down (1)

Meaning
- To stop working; to malfunction; to become inoperative; to fail to function.

Usage
- Machines and vehicles can **break down**. Any kind of mechanical device can **break down**.

Not Separable
- something **breaks down**

Examples
- The copy machine **broke down** again, so I called for service.

- The time clock in the office finally **broke down** and the boss decided not to replace it.

- The accountant likes to use an abacus because he says it never **breaks down**.

- If the forklift **breaks down** again we may need to get a new one.

- My car **broke down,** so I took the bus to work.

- Lori said her laptop **broke down,** so the boss gave her a new one

7: break down (2)

Meaning
- To analyze; to examine; to inspect; to scrutinize

Usage
- Someone can **break down** things like financial reports or a formula. In this meaning, **break down** means to analyze something in order to understand it better.

Separable
- **break down** something
- **break** something **down**

Examples
- I have to **break down** the sales figures for Friday's meeting.

- The boss asked me to **break** the report **down** for him.

- After **breaking down** the P/L statement, the accounting manager looked nervous.

- We **broke down** the check at the restaurant and discovered the waiter overcharged us.

- Jim **broke down** his household budget and realized that he couldn't afford to go on vacation this year.

- Bob **broke down** the budget but couldn't find any more items to cut.

8: break in

Meaning
- To wear something until it becomes comfortable.

Usage
- We generally use **break in** when we talk about clothing, shoes, sporting equipment, etc. which may be inflexible until it is worn or used a number of times.

Separable
- **break in** something
- **break** something **in**

Examples
- It is a nice leather jacket, but I need to **break** it **in**.

- It might take a week to **break in** these tennis shoes.

- The boss broke the window in his office when he tried to **break in** his new golf club!

- Jim got a new desk chair but it took a long time to **break** it **in**.

- I quickly **broke in** my new work shoes by visiting my customers on foot.

- Johnny **broke in** his baseball glove after a few weeks.

9: break into (1)

Meaning
- To enter a place illegally or without permission; to burglarize.

Usage
- Someone **breaks into** a place, after it is closed or when the occupants are not there, with the intention of stealing or doing damage.

Not Separable
- someone **breaks into** a place

Examples
- I heard someone **broke into** the coffee shop last night.

- Someone **broke into** my car and stole the stereo.

- Somebody **broke into** the boss's office and damaged his new computer.

- We have a high-tech security system, so it is unlikely someone will try to **break into** the office.

- Somebody **broke into** my desk last night and took my Oreo cookies.

- The police were called because someone **broke into** the warehouse.

*Note: It's also possible to use break in without a direct object:
- I forgot to lock the door. I hope no one **breaks in**.
- I lost my office key, so I had to **break in** through the window

10: break into (2)

Meaning
- To successfully enter a business, industry or sales market.

Usage
- A person can **break into** the arts or a business field. We often use **break into** when we talk about fields like show business or the music business which are difficult for most people to begin a career. A company can also **break into** a new market or sales area.

Not Separable
- someone **breaks into** a field

Examples
- Lori **broke into** the fashion industry right after graduating university.

- **Breaking into** the music business takes hard work and endurance.

- The boss gave the interns some advice about how to **break into** the advertising business.

- Jack's parents are both doctors, so it was easy for him to **break into** medicine.

- After working as a mobile phone salesman and appearing on a TV show, Paul **broke into** the music world and became a famous opera singer.

- ABC Company is trying to **break into** a new market in Taiwan.

Quiz 1

Fill in the blank space with the correct answer choice:

1. It took time, but now that I have _____ my jeans, they feel great!
    a. broken into
    b. broken down
    c. broken in
    d. backed up

2. Joe hit a police car when he _____ his car.
    a. backed away
    b. backed up
    c. blocked off
    d. broke into

3. I think two locks on the door will prevent anyone from _____ the room.
    a. breaking into
    b. breaking out
    c. breaking down
    d. breaking up

4. No matter how much he tried, Jeff couldn't _____ Broadway.
    a. break out
    b. break down
    c. break up.
    d. break into

5. The guy sitting in front of me _____ my view with his big hat.
    a. backed up
    b. backed off
    c. broke up
    d. blocked off

6. I finished my sales budget, so I need to _____ the manager after lunch.
    a. back it up
    b. break it out
    c. bounce it off
    d. block it off

7. I said I would _____ Jack if he decided to open a business.
    a. back up
    b. back into
    c. block up
    d. block off

21

8. The restaurant gave us just one receipt, so I had to _____ everyone's charges.
    a. break out   b. break down
    c. break up.   d. break into

9. Tom decided to _____ from telling his wife about plan to go to the bar.
    a. back up   b. back away
    c. break down   d. block off

10. Because the water heater _____, I had to take a cold shower.
    a. broke into   b. broke down
    c. broke in   d. broke up

Practice Section 1

Now, it's your turn to practice and use the phrasal verbs that you studied. Answer the following questions. Write a complete sentence using the given phrasal verb.

Example:
Do you know anyone who has backed away from a fight?
One of my coworkers backed away from a fight with a street vendor who tried to cheat him.

1. Do you know anyone who has **backed away** from a fight?
2. Do you need to **back** something **up** in your house?
3. Have you ever **backed** someone **up**? Has someone ever **backed** you **up**?
4. When was the last time you saw a road that was **blocked off**?
5. What idea or suggestion did you recently **bounce off** a friend, coworker, or boss?
6. Do you have anything that has **broken down** recently?
7. Have you **broken down** a report or some figures recently?
8. What have you **broken in** recently?
9. Has anyone ever **broken into** your car?
10. Would you like to **break into** the music business?

Confusing Words 1: Appointment, Reservation, Plans

We use **appointment** when we meet with a professional, like a doctor, lawyer, or the dean of a university.
- I will make an **appointment** to see the dean.
- I have an **appointment** with my dentist.

We use **reservation** for travel and entertainment, like flights, hotels, and restaurants.
- I made a **reservation** at the steak house.
- I have a hotel **reservation** for two nights.

We use **plans** when we have arrangements with friends or family. *Note that in this usage, **plans** is always plural.
- I made dinner **plans** with Jane tomorrow.
- I have **plans** to take my sister shopping.

You can use **make** + **appointment / reservation / plans** to describe the action of arranging it:
- I need to **make** an **appointment** with the dentist.
- I **made** a **reservation** for the restaurant on Friday.

You can use **have** + **appointment / reservation / plans** to describe the state or condition:
- I **have plans** with my friends this weekend.
- I **have** an **appointment** with my doctor tomorrow.

11: break out (of)

Meaning
- To escape from somewhere; to abscond; to flee.

Usage
- A person or an animal can **break out of** their confinement. We generally use **break out** when we talk about people or animals who are confined for a long time, like inmates in prison or animals in a zoo. We use **break out of** when a direct object is used.

Not Separable
- **break out (of)**

Examples
- The boss's parrot **broke out of** its cage and pooped on his desk!

- We all laughed when the mice **broke out of** their cage in the laboratory.

- The magician **broke out of** a locked safe in less than fifteen minutes.

- Nobody has ever successfully **broken out of** Alcatraz prison in San Francisco.

- The bank robber **broke out of** prison last week.

- My dog tried to **break out of** the backyard today.

---

*Note: **Break out** also means a large number of pimples appearing on your face.
- Eating those potato chips made my face **break out**.
- You face **breaks out** because you eat too much junk food!

12: break up (with)

Meaning
- To separate from someone or end a romantic relationship.

Usage
- A person can **break up** with another person. We use **break up** for both married and unmarried couples. We use **break up with** when a direct object is used.

Not Separable
- break up

Examples
- Jack **broke up with** Jane because she was cheating on him.

- When the boss found out the office manager was dating his secretary, he pressured them to **break up**.

- Tommy and Gina have a strange relationship. They have **broken up** and gotten back together three times.

- Is **breaking up** really hard to do?

- I heard Brenda **broke up with** her boyfriend.

- Suzy decided to **break up with** Jimmy after five years.

13: bring down

Meaning
- To make depressed, sad, or dispirited.

Usage
- A person or event can **bring** someone **down**. We use **bring down** to describe situations that change our feeling from happy to sad.

Separable
- **bring** someone **down**
- **bring down** someone

Examples
- Working overtime always **brings down** Ted, but he doesn't have a choice.

- Losing the big sale to our competitor **brought** everyone in the department **down**.

- I heard that rainy days and Mondays always **bring down** Karen.

- Finding out that Fey already has a boyfriend **brought** me **down**.

- The bad weather has really **brought** me **down**.

- George said sitting in heavy traffic **brings** him **down**.

14: bring up (1)

Meaning
- To mention something; to allude to; to talk about.

Usage
- A person can **bring up** a conversation topic. When someone **brings up** something, they introduce a new topic to the conversation and often what is said is not a new topic. We also use **bring up** to mention unpleasant topics.

Separable
- **bring** something **up**
- **bring up** something

Examples
- The boss **brought** up Jack's persistent lateness in the meeting.

- My high school friends often **bring up** embarrassing things that we did when we were younger.

- I'm sorry to **bring** this **up**, but your zipper is open.

- Please don't **bring up** how drunk I was last night to my wife!

- At the party, Tony **brought up** his new job.

- Frank always **brings** his ex-girlfriends **up** when he meets a new girl.

15: bring up (2)

Meaning
- To raise (children); to parent; to rear (children).

Usage
- A parent or caregiver can **bring up** a child. Children are **brought up** in a certain place or in a certain way.

Separable
- **bring** someone **up**
- **bring up** someone

Examples

- Fay's amazing mother **brought** her **up** at a time when single mothers were not so common.

- My grandparents **brought up** five children during the Great Depression of the 1930's.

- Were you **brought up** in the city or the countryside?

- They **brought up** their kids with strict discipline.

- My parents **brought** me **up** in New York.

- Brad is **bringing** his kids **up** nicely.

16: butt in / into

Meaning
- To interrupt when others are speaking.

Usage
- A person can **butt in** when another person is talking, or a person can **butt into** a conversation. We use **butt into** when a direct object is used.

Not Separable
- **butt in**
- **butt into**

Examples
- Tom! Please don't **butt in** when I am talking.

- It is rude to **butt in** when another person is speaking.

- I don't like attending meetings with Joe. He often **butts in** and disturbs our discussions.

- Don't **butt into** our conversation. This doesn't pertain to you.

- Serena always **butts into** the conversation. It's very annoying.

- If you **butt into** the conversation once more, I'm going to punch you!

17: call back

Meaning

- To return a telephone call. To telephone someone who had telephoned you.

Usage

- A person can **call back someone** who just called them. If you miss someone's call, you will **call them back**.

Separable

- **call** someone **back**
- **call back** someone

Examples

- [Voicemail message] At the sound of the tone, please leave your name and phone number, and I will **call you back** when I return to the office.

- Thanks for **calling back**.

- My ex-girlfriend called and left a message asking me to **call** her **back**. I wonder why...

- I tried to **call back** Jack, but the line was busy for two hours.

- I need to **call** my sister **back**.

- Did you **call back** the technician about your computer?

18: call off

Meaning
- To cancel; to scrap; to axe.

Usage
- A person can **call off** a scheduled event. When something is **called off**, it is cancelled.

Separable
- **call** something **off**
- **call off** something

Examples
- We have to **call off** the meeting tomorrow because the CEO has an urgent matter to take care of.

- The company **called off** its plans to rent additional space.

- Rachel **called** the wedding **off** one day before the ceremony!

- I refuse to **call off** our trip to Disneyland just because your mother wants to visit us that weekend! She should come another time.

- We **called off** the golf game due to the bad weather.

- I don't want to **call** the party **off**, even though it is snowing.

19: call on

Meaning
- To visit a person.

Usage
- A person can **call on** another person. **Call on** can be used in both personal and business situations. Note that **call on** means to visit in person, face-to-face, and not by using the telephone.

Not Separable
- **call on**

Examples
- The pesky salesman **calls on** us every month, even though we never buy anything from him.

- Aunt Betty was so happy when we **called on** her last week.

- I **called on** Jim's clients when he was out of town on vacation.

- I heard the CEO is going to **call on** us sometime next week. I wonder why.

- I **called on** Steve when I was in Miami.

- We **call on** our good customers once a month.

20: call up

Meaning
- To telephone someone.

Usage
- A person can **call up** another person. **Call up** always means to contact someone by telephone, not face-to-face.

Separable
- **call** someone **up**
- **call up** someone

Examples
- We tried **calling up** all of our old customers in order to make some sales.

- Can you call back Jack? He **called up** while you were in the meeting.

- The same pesky salesman **called** me **up** three times this month!

- I **called up** Jane to invite her to the party but she wasn't home.

- Did you **call up** the doctor to make an appointment?

- Aunt Jane **called** me **up** last night.

Quiz 2

Fill in the blank space with the correct answer choice:

1. Suddenly having to work on Saturday _____.
    a. brought me up   b. broke me out
    c. broke me up   d. brought me down

2. I don't want to _____ my ex-wife, but I need to pick up my golf clubs.
    a. call on   b. call off
    c. clean up   d. calm down

3. Taka was born in Japan and _____ in New York City.
    a. brought up   b. brought down
    c. broken into   d. broken out

4. I forgot to _____ my girlfriend and she got mad at me.
    a. calm down   b. bring down
    c. call off   d. call back

5. We need to _____ everybody in the family to tell them the good news.
    a. break up   b. break out
    c. call up   d. call off

6. I told Tommy to _____ with Jane because she's a heartbreaker.
    a. bring up   b. back up
    c. break up   d. bring down

7. Mom! Stop _____ embarrassing stories in front of my friends!
    a. bringing up   b. breaking out
    c. bringing down   d. calling up

35

8. Tom _____ the party because of the heavy snowstorm.
    a. called up   b. called back
    c. called on   d. called off

9. The prisoners planned to _____ after dinner.
    a. break out   b. back away
    c. break in   d. back up

10. Why do you always _____ when I am talking?
    a. break in   b. butt in
    c. call up   d. bring down

Practice Section 2

Now, it's your turn to practice and use the phrasal verbs that you studied. Answer the following questions. Write a complete sentence using the given phrasal verb.

1. Does your pet, or your neighbor's pet try to **break out of** the yard?

2. Do you know someone who has **broken up with** someone recently?

3. What **brings** you **down**?

4. Do you have a friend that **brings up** something from the past?

5. Do you know anyone who is **bringing up** their kids right now?

6. Do you have a friend or coworker who **butts in** to a conversation?

7. Who did you **call back** today?

8. Have you ever **called off** anything because of the weather?

9. How often do you **call on** someone? Who is it?

10. Have you **called up** someone recently?

Confusing Words 2: Borrow vs. Lend

Borrow

We use **borrow** when we use another person's something for a short amount of time. There are two basic grammar patterns with the same meaning. Borrow is a regular verb, so the three forms are **borrow**, **borrowed**, and **borrowed**.

The first pattern is [someone] **borrows** [something] from [someone].
- I **borrowed** a pen from George.
- Jack often **borrows** books from his father.

The next pattern is [someone] **borrows** [somebody's something].
- I **borrowed** George's pen.
- Jack often **borrows** his father's books.

When you need something, you can ask this way:
- Can I **borrow** your pen?

Lend

When you **lend** something, you give it to someone for a short amount of time. There are two basic grammar patterns with the same meaning. **Lend** is an irregular verb, so the three forms are **lend**, **lent**, and **lent**.

The first pattern is [someone] **lends** [something] to [someone].
- George **lent** a pen to me.
- Jack's father often **lends** books to him.

The next pattern is [someone] lends [someone]. [something].
- George always **lends** me a pen.
- Jack's father often **lends** him books.

When you need something, you can ask this way:
- Can you **lend** me a pen?

21: calm down

Meaning
- To relax; to soothe.

Usage
- A person can **calm down**, or something can **calm** a person **down**. When someone is upset or agitated, you can **calm** them **down** or they can **calm down**.

Separable
- **calm down**
- **calm** someone **down**
- **calm down** someone

Examples
- I know you are upset. Try to **calm down** and tell me what happened.

- Every night, Jack has a glass of brandy to help him **calm down** after work.

- Even though coffee has caffeine, it **calms** me **down**.

- After we told the kids we were going to Disneyland, they couldn't **calm down**.

- The police tried to **calm** her **down** after the accident.

- Classical music really **calms** me **down**.

22: cheer up

Meaning

- To make someone who is sad feel better.
- To perk up; to brighten (a person's mood)

Usage

- A person/something can **cheer** someone **up**, or a person/something can **cheer up** a person.

Separable

- **cheer up**
- **cheer** someone **up**
- **cheer up** someone

Examples

- Do you know a good way to **cheer up** a person with a broken heart?

- Listening to those old songs on the radio always **cheers** me **up**.

- **Cheer up**, Jack. I'm sure you'll find your lost dog.

- I don't care what you say. Nothing can **cheer** me **up** now. Go away!

- I brought some flowers to **cheer** my mother **up**.

- Our visit with grandma really **cheered** her **up**.

23: clam up

Meaning
- To stop talking

Usage
- A person can **clam up**.

Not Separable
- **clam up**

Examples
- I wanted to disagree with the boss during the meeting, but I just **clammed up**.

- The manager told Tony to **clam up** because he was chatting too much during work.

- Why don't you just **clam up**. You are talking too much.

- Ok, everybody **clam up**! We cannot accomplish anything if everyone talks at once.

- I **clammed up** when she told me the shocking news.

- Jake said he **clammed up** when the other guys started talking about the Yankee game, because he doesn't follow sports.

24: clean up

Meaning
- To clean or organize something or somewhere completely.

Usage
- A person can **clean up** something or somewhere.

Separable
- **clean up**
- **clean** something **up**
- **clean up** something

Examples
- The CEO is coming tomorrow, so we had better **clean up** the office.

- I found my lost car keys when I **cleaned up** the office.

- Jane said she spends the whole day **cleaning up** after her three kids.

- Well, we cooked, ate, and then **cleaned up** the kitchen. Let's relax now.

- Please **clean up** this room. It is so messy.

- Have you **cleaned** the garage **up** yet?

25: clear up

Meaning
- To solve or resolve.

Usage
- A person can **clear up** something, or **clear** something **up**.

Separable
- **clear** something **up**
- **clear up** something

Examples
- Were you able to **clear up** the problem with the computer?

- At the meeting we tried to **clear up** the misunderstanding that we had with our customer.

- I need to **clear up** some of the errors in the accounting report.

- Can you help me **clear** something **up**?

- Jane said she has to **clear** a few problems **up**, so she asked me to have a meeting this afternoon.

- We've already **cleared** that issue **up**. Why is it on the meeting agenda?

26: count on

Meaning
- To depend on; to rely on.

Usage
- A person can **count on** another person or a thing.

Not Separable
- **count on**

Examples
- The boss is **counting on** us to finish the project on time.

- We can always **count on** Jack to work hard.

- Jim said he is **counting on** winning the lottery to pay his bills. How foolish!

- The whole team is **counting on** the pitcher to win the game.

- I am **counting on** you to do your homework.

- The museum is **counting on** donations from its patrons.

27: cut down (on)

Meaning
- To reduce the intake of something; to decrease

Usage
- A person can **cut down on** food, drink, or doing something. We use **cut down on** when a direct object is used.

Not Separable
- **cut down (on)**

Examples
- The boss told Joe to **cut down on** using facebook in the office.

- I play pachinko too often. I should **cut down**.

- The doctor told Saori to **cut down on** coffee.

- We need to **cut down on** using paper to help the environment.

- I have to **cut down on** eating junk food.

- Jack is trying to **cut down on** smoking.

28: cut out

Meaning
- To stop doing something; to eliminate

Usage
- A person can cut out a food, drink, or doing something.

Separable
- **cut** something **out**
- **cut out** something

Examples
- I want to **cut out** working overtime, but my boss is too strict.

- Jack said that in his office, they **cut out** using color photocopies to save money.

- The company cafeteria **cut out** serving donuts in the afternoon.

- I started eating a lot when I **cut out** smoking.

- Lucy **cut** fried foods **out** of her diet.

- The doctor told me to exercise and **cut out** snacks.

29: drag on

Meaning
- To continue for an unnecessarily long time.

Usage
- A person or a thing can **drag on**.

Not Separable
- **drag on**

Examples
- The boss's presentations always **drag on** and make us sleepy.

- Jack's explanation about why he was late **dragged on**, so the boss looked irritated.

- The move I saw last night was too long. It **dragged on** for almost three hours.

- It's only 1:00pm. This day is **dragging on**.

- Bob's speech **dragged on** for two hours.

- The labor strike has **dragged on** for several weeks.

30: dress up

Meaning
- To wear fancy or formal clothing; to dress stylishly.

Usage
- A person **dresses up** for special occasions. A person can **dress up** another person.

Separable
- **dress up**
- **dress** someone **up**
- **dress up** someone

Examples
- I used to **dress up** to go to the office, but in my new company, everyone wears casual clothes.

- We **dressed up** because some of the directors were visiting the office.

- Jane looks very pretty when she **dresses up**.

- My wife likes to **dress up** and enjoy afternoon tea with her friends.

- I like to **dress up** when I go out to eat.

- Ken **dressed** his daughter **up** for the party.

Quiz 3

Fill in the blank space with the correct answer choice:

1. I know you are upset, but you'd better_____. Don't start a fight with him now.
    - a. clam up
    - b. clean up
    - c. drag on
    - d. cheer up

2. I wasn't able to _____ the issues in this report. Can you help me?
    - a. clam up
    - b. count on
    - c. calm down
    - d. clear up

3. _____! You're going to find a better girlfriend soon!
    - a. Count on
    - b. Call up
    - c. Dress up
    - d. Cheer up

4. The medicine finally helped her to _____.
    - a. call back
    - b. dress up
    - c. clam up
    - d. calm down

5. Ever since he _____ smoking, the boss has been in a bad mood.
    - a. cut out
    - b. counted on
    - c. cleaned up
    - d. cheered up

6. Koji said he can't _____ eating hot dogs. He loves them!
    - a. clam up
    - b. drag on
    - c. count on
    - d. cut down on

7. The boss made us _____ in our suits when we attended the baseball game!
    - a. cut out
    - b. dress up
    - c. clean up
    - d. drag on

49

8. My boss's golf stories _____ for way too long.
    a. dress up   b. drag on
    c. cut down on   d. count on

9. If I don't _____ the garage, I'll never find my tools.
    a. drag on   b. cut out
    c. cheer up   d. clean up

10. No bonus this year? I was _____ the bonus for my vacation!
    a. cutting down on   b. cutting out
    c. counting on   d. cheering up

Practice Section 3

Now, it's your turn to practice and use the phrasal verbs that you studied. Answer the following questions. Write a complete sentence using the given phrasal verb.

1. What kind of music **calms** you **down**?

2. Who have you **cheered up** recently?

3. When was the last time you told someone to **clam up?**

4. What have you **cleaned up** recently?

5. Have you needed to **clear up** any problems in your office or at home recently?

6. What are you **counting on**?

7. Are you trying to **cut down on** something?

8. Have you **cut out** anything from your diet?

9. Has anything **dragged on** around you recently?

10. When was the last time you **dressed up**?

Confusing Words 3: During vs. While

During

We use **during** + [noun*] to show something that happens (or doesn't happen) in a situation or time period.
- I don't use my cell phone **during** work.
- I always listen to the radio **during** my commute.
- Jack watches TV **during** dinner.

*Note: Don't use **during** + gerund (the ING verb participle). For example, you can say, "**during** work" but not "**during** working."

While

We use **while** + [subject] + [verb] to show two actions that happen (or don't happen) at the same time.
- I don't use my cell phone **while** I am working.
- I always listen to the radio **while** I am driving to work.
- Jack watches TV **while** he is eating dinner.

We also use **while** + [gerund] with the same meaning
- I don't use my cell phone **while** working.
- I always listen to the radio **while** driving to work.
- Jack watches TV **while** eating dinner.

31: drop by

Meaning
- To visit a person or a place for a short time.

Usage
- A person **drops by** somewhere and stays for a short time.

Not Separable
- **drop by**

Examples
- Jack from ABC Company **dropped by** the office to see you.

- I always **drop by** the coffee shop on my way to work.

- Before we reach conference center, I need to **drop by** the convenience store.

- I want to **drop by** the post office after work.

- I'm going to **drop by** Albert's house after work.

- Bill said he will **drop by** here on his way to the airport.

32: drop off

Meaning
- To bring and unload something or someone.

Usage
- A person can **drop off** someone or something in or at some place.

Separable
- **drop** someone/something **off**
- **drop off** someone/something

Examples
- Bob **dropped off** his laptop at the IT department because it needed repair.

- Someone needs to **drop off** Jack at the airport.

- The taxi driver **dropped** me **off** right in front of the hotel.

- I think I forgot my keys at the library when I **dropped off** my books.

- I need to **drop off** my shirts at the dry cleaners.

- Judy **drops** the kids **off** at school on her way to work.

33: eat out

Meaning
- To eat a meal at a restaurant instead of at home.

Usage
- A person can **eat out**.
- You can also **eat** [breakfast / lunch / dinner] **out**.

Separable
- eat out
- eat [meal] out

Examples
- On Wednesdays, we don't work overtime, so my team members always **eat out** together.

- In New York City, it is a bit expensive to **eat** lunch **out** every day, so I bring my lunch to save money.

- Jane said she prefers cooking at home to **eating out**.

- My wife doesn't want to cook tonight, so we are going to **eat** dinner **out**.

- We like to **eat out** on Friday nights.

- Lenny said he **ate out** at that new Italian restaurant on 32nd Street.

34: fall through

Meaning
- To fail; to be unsuccessful

Usage
- [something] **falls through.** Things like plans, arrangements, or negotiations can **fall through**.

Not Separable
- **fall through**

Examples
- Jack's appointment to a management position **fell through** because of a lack of support from the HR director.

- We need to work extra hard to make sure this deal does not **fall through**.

- If your plans to go on a date with Jane **fall through**, let me know. I'm free on Friday night.

- The negotiations between my company and ABC company **fell through**.

- My plans to vacation in Mexico **fell through**.

- Bob's dream of buying a boat **fell through** when he got laid off.

35: figure out

Meaning
- To solve or understand the solution to something.

Usage
- A person can **figure out** something. We usually use **figure out** when we talk about finding the solution to a problem, a difficult situation, or a mathematical equation.

Separable
- **figure** something **out**
- **figure out** something

Examples
- We've tried lowering our prices and offering more products, but sales are still not good. I can't **figure out** what the customers want!

- I always get lost in Shibuya station in Tokyo. I can't **figure out** which exit to use.

- Can you help me? I can't **figure out** how to make my wife happy.

- The boss wants us to **figure out** how to expand our business in Asia.

- I need to **figure out** these math equations that the teacher gave us.

- Kris is having trouble **figuring** his homework **out**.

36: fill in

Meaning
- To handwrite or enter information in a designated space.

Usage
- A person can **fill in** information (such as their name, address, etc.) somewhere.

Separable
- **fill** something **in**
- **fill in** something

Examples
- After you **fill in** your name and email address, click the "submit" button.

- If you do not **fill in** all of the required information, you cannot submit the application form.

- Just **fill in** your name and date of birth, and the doctor will be right with you.

- You can **fill in** your work history, or just include your resume with this application form.

- Please **fill** your information **in** on this form.

- You need to **fill in** your order on the paper and give it to the cashier.

37: fill out

Meaning
- To complete a document such as a form or survey.

Usage
- A person can **fill out** a survey, an application, a form, etc.

Separable
- **fill** something **out**
- **fill out** something

Examples
- You need to **fill out** the customs form completely before shipping the package.

- I **filled out** the "vacation request form," but the boss hasn't approved it yet.

- All visitors to the office need to **fill out** a short survey before they can talk with a counselor.

- My application was rejected because I didn't **fill out** the correct form.

- I **filled out** a job application at the coffee shop.

- **Fill** the warrantee card **out** completely before mailing it.

38: fill up

Meaning
- To make something completely full.

Usage
- A person can **fill up** a container like a bag, a suitcase, etc.

Separable
- **fill** something **up**
- **fill up** something

Examples
- I **filled up** two boxes with brochures for the exhibition.

- Jack **filled up** two plates with food at the breakfast buffet. I wonder how he will eat all of it!

- The receptionist **filled up** the customer's coffee to the top of the cup.

- If you **fill** your backpack **up** with books, it will be too heavy to carry.

- Jane **filled up** two suitcases with stuff she bought in Spain.

- We should **fill** our water bottles **up** before continuing our hike.

39: find out

Meaning
- To discover new information by either searching for it or being informed or notified.

Usage
- A person can **find out** something or find something out.

Separable
- **find** something **out**
- **find out** something

Examples
- If the boss **finds out** you are dating his secretary, he will get very angry with you!

- I want to **find out** why Jack got fired.

- The accounting department **found out** Joe used the company credit card for some personal purchases.

- I wasn't able to **find out** how my grandparents met each other.

- I **found out** my grandmother worked in a restaurant.

- If you want to **find** the information **out**, you need to check with the receptionist.

What's the difference: **Find vs. Find Out?**

You **FIND** an *object*...but...
You **FIND OUT** some *information*.

- I found a dollar on the street!
- I found out my grandpa was a chef.

40: flip out (over)

Meaning
- To react to something in a shocked way.

Usage
- We usually use **flip out** to show someone's shocked response to something. When we use a direct object, we use **flip out over**

Not Separable
- flip out
- flip out over

Examples
- The boss **flipped out** when Jack came to the office late again today.

- My wife **flipped out** when I told her I am being transferred to work in the New York branch office for six months.

- When the boss **finds out** we didn't get the contract signed, he is going to flip out.

- Jane **flipped out over** the news that her company was moving from New York to Oklahoma.

- Fred **flipped out over** the car accident.

- If your girlfriend finds out you went to a club last night, she will **flip out**!

Quiz 4

Fill in the blank space with the correct answer choice:

1. I'm surprised that Jim can afford to _____ every night.
    - a. drag on
    - b. clean up
    - c. eat out
    - d. drop by

2. What time are you going to _____ the office tomorrow?
    - a. cut down on
    - b. drop off
    - c. fall through
    - d. drop by

3. I think if this deal _____, someone is going to get fired.
    - a. cuts down
    - b. cleans up
    - c. falls through
    - d. cuts out

4. I _____ Jane at her house after work.
    - a. dropped off
    - b. fell through
    - c. cut out
    - d. cleaned up

5. You have to _____ your employer's address and phone number on the application.
    - a. fill up
    - b. find out
    - c. fill in
    - d. figure out

6. My wife will _____ if I come home drunk.
    - a. get into
    - b. fill up
    - c. fall through
    - d. flip out

7. Jack _____ our glasses of beer all night at the bar.
    - a. filled out
    - b. filled up
    - c. filled in
    - d. found out

8. You can _____ a good deal of information online these days.
    a. get into
    b. fill up
    c. find out
    d. fall through

9. I _____ the registration card and handed it to her.
    a. gave away
    b. figured out
    c. found out
    d. filled out

10. I can't _____ why this coffee maker doesn't work.
    a. fill in
    b. figure out
    c. fill out
    d. flip out

Practice Section 4

Now, it's your turn to practice and use the phrasal verbs that you studied. Answer the following questions. Write a complete sentence using the given phrasal verb.

1. Have you **dropped by** somewhere recently?

2. Have you **dropped off** something or someone recently?

3. Where do you like to **eat out**?

4. Has something **fallen though** recently?

5. Have you had any trouble **figuring** something **out**?

6. What have you **filled in** the search engine box recently?

7. Have you **filled out** any forms recently?

8. Have you **filled up** any containers recently?

9. What have you **found out** recently?

10. When was the last time you **flipped out**? What did you **flip out over**?

Confusing Words 4: Taste and Flavor

Taste

We use the noun form of **taste** to talk about food, and usually we use **taste** when we talk about one general type of food.
- Too much salt will ruin the **taste** of that steak.
- I like the **taste** of that ice cream.

We also use the verb form of **taste**, which relates to the sense of **taste** we have in our mouth.
- Thai curry **tastes** delicious.
- Chocolate and potato chips **taste** great together.

Flavor

We use the noun form of **flavor**, which refers to your reaction to the ingredients in food, such as a special dish that has been made. For this reason, it is more common to use **flavor** than **taste** when we talk about dishes or other prepared food.
- The **flavor** of this pizza is just amazing.
- The food in that restaurant has true Japanese **flavor**.

We also use **flavor** when we talk about different kinds of the same food. For example:
- Which ice cream **flavor** do you like - chocolate or vanilla?
- This soda comes in several **flavors**, including cherry, orange, and grape.

We also use the verb form of **flavor**, which means "to season." For example:
- The chef **flavors** the soup with salt and bay leaves.
- My mom **flavors** her pasta sauce with garlic.

41: freak out

Meaning
- To become angry or upset.

Usage
- A person can **freak out** when they hear or discover bad or shocking news.

Not Separable
- **freak out**

Examples
- The CEO **freaked out** when he saw the poor sales results from last quarter.

- Mike's wife **freaked out** when she saw him in a café with a beautiful woman.

- I **freaked out** when I found out someone dented my car.

- Don't **freak out**, ok? I have some bad news.

- Jen **freaked out** when her friend came to the party wearing the same dress.

- If your husband finds out that you bought an expensive bag he's gonna **freak out**.

42: get away (from)

Meaning
- To escape; to break free

Usage
- A person or an animal can **get away** from somewhere or something. We can also use **get away** to mean leave an emotional situation. We use **get away from** when a direct object is used.

Not Separable
- **get away (from)**

Examples
- There was a mouse in the office. We tried to catch it, but it **got away**.

- I have too much work to do today, so I can't **get away** to have lunch.

- I've been working hard for the past few months. I need to take a break and **get away from** work for a while.

- You can't **get away from** going to the second party tonight. Let's go!

- The cat **got away from** its owner and ran up the hill.

- The robber tried to **get away**, but eventually he was caught.

43: get into

Meaning
- To become interested in (doing) something. To begin liking (to do) something.

Usage
- A person can **get into** a kind of entertainment, sport, food, etc.

Not Separable
- **get into**

Examples
- Jack said he can't **get into** his new position as a salesman.

- Yoko really **got into** living in New York when she met her boyfriend.

- How did you **get into** playing shogi?

- Yumi **got into** baking bread and cake so much that she decided to open a bakery.

- I **got into** jazz when I was in college.

- Gene **got into** exercising when he married a fitness instructor.

44: get out of

Meaning
- To escape from a situation, contract, agreement, etc.
- To become uninvolved in a situation.

Usage
- **Get out of** gives us the idea that someone, an animal, or a business is in an undesirable situation and wishes to escape from that situation. We generally use **get out of** to show that someone wants to separate himself or herself from a situation.

Not Separable
- **get out of**

Examples
- Everyone is supposed to go to the pub after work with the boss, so I think it would be impossible to **get out of** it.

- Jack said he is trying to **get out of** his relationship with Jane, but she won't stop calling him.

- I have an appointment to meet the lawyer. We are trying to **get out of** the ten-year contract with Acme Employment Corp.

- Dianne finally **got out of** her bad marriage to Joe.

- ABC company is trying to **get out of** the business deal they made with XYZ.

- Kevin wants to **get out of** his lease, but the landlord refused.

45: give away

Meaning
- To distribute for free.

Usage
- A person or a business can give something away.

Separable
- **give** something **away**
- **give away** something

Examples
- Greg **gave away** cigars when his son was born.

- In some cities, they **give away** pocket tissues with advertising near the train stations.

- The department store is having a raffle drawing to **give away** five $100 gift certificates.

- I want to **give away** my old clothes to charity.

- The bookstore is **giving** calendars **away** to its customers.

- When Debbie moved, she **gave** all of her furniture **away**.

We also use **giveaway** as a noun. In this way, **giveaway** means the item that is given:

- A pen is a common **giveaway** in business
- What kind of **giveaway** should we prepare for the next promotion?

46: give in/into

Meaning
- To yield; to surrender; to capitulate.

Usage
- A person can **give in**. We use **give in** when a person capitulates to doing something that they really didn't want to do or think of doing. We use **give into** when a direct object is used. *(Give in to is also a possible spelling.)*

Not Separable
- **give in**
- **give into**

Examples
- I asked the boss to let me go home early on Friday, but he wouldn't **give in**.

- My wife finally **gave in** when I asked her to let me go to Las Vegas with my friends.

- No matter how much you ask me to taste natto, I won't **give in**.

- Jack **gave into** his wife and bought her a designer brand bag.

- The mother **gave into** her son's begging for a cookie.

- The government **gave into** the demonstrators' demands for the president to resign.

47: give up

Meaning
- To surrender; to quit

Usage
- A person or a group of people can **give up**, when they realize that there is no alternative. We also use **give up** to mean quit, especially to quit a habit.

Separable
- **give** something **up**
- **give up** something

Examples
- We must not **give up** trying to reach the financial targets.

- After several months of phone calls and emails, the salesman **gave up** trying to make us buy his copy machine.

- The boss **gave up** making us work on Saturdays when we all complained to HR about it.

- The team didn't **give up** trying to climb the mountain, even though the weather was bad.

- I **gave up** playing baseball when I was twenty-five.

- Rachel tried to **give** smoking **up** several times.

48: go over

Meaning
- To review; to examine.

Usage
- A person or a group of people can go over something.

Not Separable
- **go over**

Examples
- I want to **go over** this contract with you before we sign it.

- We need to **go over** next week's meeting agenda.

- Jack will **go over** the plans with us tomorrow.

- We **went over** the script several times before it was printed.

- We will **go over** the presentation once more before the meeting.

- I **went over** my itinerary several times before my trip to Dubai.

49: go under

Meaning
- To go bankrupt

Usage
- A business can **go und**er. When a business goes bankrupt, we say it **goes under**.

Not Separable
- [company] goes under

Examples
- We have to have a strategy to prevent the company from **going under**.

- Jack's company is one of the few advertising agencies that hasn't been acquired or **gone under**.

- When Mike's company **went under**, he decided to start his own business.

- **Going under** is not an option. We need to cut costs and increase sales.

- If we don't improve the cash flow, we risk **going under**.

- Many new businesses **go under** because they don't have a realistic business plan.

50: grow up

Meaning
- To mature, to spend one's childhood.

Usage
- A person can **grow up** in a place or in a certain way. Note that we only use **grow up** for people, not plants or animals.

Not Separable
- **grow up**

Examples
- The new boss was born in Sapporo, but **grew up** in California.

- Where did you **grow up**?

- Jack still drinks milk with his lunch. I guess he hasn't **grown up** yet.

- Vincent lived in Paris when he was **growing up**.

- Did you know Bon Jovi **grew up** in New Jersey?

- Bob's daughter **grew up** to be a successful doctor.

---

*Note the difference between **grow** and **grow up**. **Grow** means to become bigger, **grow up** means to mature. *Only* people **grow up**.
- My tomato plants are **growing** nicely.
- We **grew up** in a small town.

Quiz 5

Fill in the blank space with the correct answer choice:

1. It's hard to _____ from the office before 5:00pm.
    a. get out of   b. get away
    c. get into   d. give away

2. Joe wants to _____ his relationship with Carol because she is not his type.
    a. give away   b. get away
    c. get into   d. get out of

3. I _____ that movie because the story is fantastic.
    a. got away   b. gave in
    c. got into   d. got out of

4. Some guy on Fifth Ave was _____ dollar bills!
    a. giving away   b. giving in
    c. giving up   d. going over

5. The boss will certainly _____ if Tony is late for work again today.
    a. give up   b. freak out
    c. go over   d. get out of

6. My wife won't _____, so no trip to Vegas for me. She's too stubborn.
    a. give up   b. give in
    c. grow up   d. go over

7. When we _____ the initiations, we realized we forgot to invite Jack.
    a. gave in   b. gave up
    c. grew up   d. went over

8. I heard that Tony _____ with his grandmother in Spain.
    a. gave in   b. went under
    c. grew up   d. got away

9. The business _____ after it was sued.
    a. gave into   b. went under
    c. gave away   d. went over

10. I think I need to _____ eating so much pizza. I've been putting on weight recently.
    a. freak out   b. grow up
    c. give up   d. get out of

Practice Section 5

Now, it's your turn to practice and use the phrasal verbs that you studied. Answer the following questions. Write a complete sentence using the given phrasal verb.

1. Did anything make you **freak out** recently?

2. If you were on a deserted island, how would you **get away**?

3. What have you **gotten into** recently?

4. Have you ever needed to get out of something?

5. Have you **given** anything **away** recently?

6. Have you **given into** something or someone recently?

7. Have you ever tried to **give** something **up**?

8. What have you **gone over** recently?

9. What can a company in your industry do to prevent itself from **going under**?

10. Do you know someone who **grew up** to be successful?

Confusing Words 5: Cost, Spend, & Take

Cost

We use **cost** to talk about the required amount of money of something.
- At the beach, a hot dog **costs** around five dollars.
- An iPad **costs** less in New York than it does in Tokyo.

We also use **cost** to complain about a situation in which we feel that we wasted our time doing something.
- That meeting **cost** me three hours. Now I need to work overtime.
- The traffic jam **cost** me an extra half an hour this morning.

Spend

We use **spend** to talk about using both money and time.
- I **spent** an hour in a traffic jam this morning.
- We **spend** three hundred dollars a month on groceries.

Take

We use **take** to talk about using time.
- It **takes** about 20 minutes to get from home to school.
- Flying from New York to São Paulo **takes** about twelve hours.

EXTRA!

We use *How long does it take?* when we want to know the amount of time needed do something.

Chris: How long does it take to bake homemade bread?
Ted: It **takes*** about 4 hours.
Chris: Wow! It only takes 10 minutes to buy some!
*Not, ~~I take~~

51: hang around / out

Meaning
- To spend relaxing time.

Usage
- A person can **hang around** in a place or with someone else. **Hang around** and **hang out** have the same meaning. We often use **hang around** + a place and **hang out with** + a person

Not Separable
- **hang around** [somewhere]
- **hang out** [somewhere]
- **hang out with** [a person]

Examples
- I was **hanging around** the office while waiting for Jack to finish his meeting.

- I'll be finished with my work in twenty minutes. Can you **hang around** for a while, or do you have to leave?

- After work let's **hang out** with Jack and Tony. They know some good places to go.

- There are some strange guys **hanging around** the subway station.

- Frank likes to **hang out** with his friends at the pizza shop on the weekends.

- Jimmy was **hanging around** with a bad group of kids.

52: hang on (to)

Meaning
- To grasp something; to take hold of something.

Usage
- A person can **hang on** or **hang on to** something. **Hang on** is used to describe the physical action of holding something. We use **hang on to** when a direct object is used.

Not Separable
- **hang on**
- **hang on to** [something / someone]

Examples
- You are supposed to **hang on to** the pole when you ride the subway.

- **Hang on to** this rope. I will help you get into the boat.

- The squirrel **hung on to** the tree with his sharp claws.

- It looks like the road ahead is rough. Please fasten your seatbelts and **hang on to** the handles.

- When you go on the rollercoaster, do you usually **hang on**, or put your hands in the air?

- I was **hanging on to** the steering wheel of the car tightly during the snowstorm.

53: hold back (from)

Meaning
- To restrain from doing something.

Usage
- A person or a business can **hold back** something or **hold back from** doing something.

Not Separable
- **hold back** something
- **hold back from** doing

Examples
- The boss wants us to **hold back from** paying the ABC Company invoice until they ship all of the items.

- It is better to **hold back** your thoughts than to say something that might offend someone.

- Jane **held back** her tears when she told us the bad news.

- Please don't **hold back**. Tell me exactly what you think.

- I **held back from** saying something to him, even though I was angry.

- The company **held back from** paying its bills due to its cash flow problems.

54: hold on (for)

Meaning
- To wait, generally for a short time.

Usage
- A person can **hold on** the phone, or in person, or for a period of time. **Hold on** is often used on the telephone and in face to face conversations when you want the other person to wait. **Hold on for** is used when the waiting time period is mentioned.

Not Separable
- **hold on**
- **hold on (for)**

Examples
- Can you **hold on for** a moment? I'll tell Mr. Jones you have arrived.

- I can't **hold on for** very long, so I think I will call you back.

- You'd like to speak to Jack? Ok, please **hold on** while I try his extension.

- I don't like listening to the background music when I am **holding on** the phone.

- I had to **hold on** while the receptionist took another call.

- The man at the bank made me **hold on for** ten minutes.

55: hold on to

Meaning
- To grasp something. (1) To take hold of some physical object; (2) To cling to a feeling, hope, or some other abstract emotional thing.

Usage
- A person can **hold on to** something physical such as a handle, or **hold on to** something emotionally, such as a memory.

Not Separable
- **hold on to**

Examples
- (1) Children must **hold on to** the handle when riding the escalator.

- (1) You'd better **hold on to** the railing of the boat tightly. Here comes another wave.

- (1) **Hold on to** the pole when you ride the subway.

- (2) The boss is **holding on to** hope that we can sign the contract with ABC Company.

- (2) Business is not good these days and sales are down, but we are still **holding on to** our belief that things will improve.

- (2) Jane is **holding on to** the good memories of her childhood.

56: hook up (with)

Meaning
- To connect with someone for fun or romance.

Usage
- Two people can **hook up**. **Hook up** is used when one person (or group) connects and gets involved with another person (or group). We use **hook up with** when a direct object is used.

Not Separable
- **hook up**
- **hook up with**

Examples
- A networking event is a good place to **hook up with** potential customers.

- It seems like Jack **hooked up with** the new receptionist in the office. They are always chatting very closely.

- I **hooked up with** my coworkers last night for a round of golf.

- I heard Paul McCartney **hooked up with** John Lennon when they were in art school.

- You like Jazz? You should **hook up with** my friend Joe. He loves jazz too.

- Do you want to **hook up** after work for a drink?

57: keep on

Meaning
- To continue doing something.

Usage
- A person or a group of people can **keep on** doing something. We generally use **keep on** + a gerund.

Not Separable
- **keep on**

Examples
- The boss wants us to **keep on** studying English until we can get a 900 on the TOEIC.

- Please **keep on** trying to convince ABC Company to buy our products.

- I think we can't **keep on** using these old computers. Let's talk to the boss about getting new ones.

- We can't **keep on** having this secret love affair. If the boss finds out, we may get fired.

- I need to **keep on** studying English in order to speak more fluently.

- If you **keep on** eating junk food, you'll gain a lot of weight.

58: kick back (at/in)

Meaning
- To relax.

Usage
- A person can **kick back** at or in a place. Kick back is used to mean relax and is often used in the set phrase, "kick back and relax."

Not Separable
- **kick back (at/in)**

Examples
- Even though we signed the contract, we can't **kick back** and relax now. We must still work hard to ensure customer satisfaction.

- The boss was angry when he saw Jack **kicking back** and watching videos on his computer during work.

- We will have three days of very busy meetings. Then we can **kick back** on the weekend.

- Ah, Sunday afternoon. I think I will **kick back** and watch the football game.

- I was **kicking back** at the bar last night with my friends.

- On the weekend I like to **kick back** at home.

59: kick off

Meaning
- To start or begin something that has a starting or ending time.

Usage
- A person can **kick off** an event like a show, a game, a meeting, etc.

Not Separable
- **kick off**

Examples
- We **kicked off** yesterday's meeting with a speech by the CEO.

- Jack said his company **kicked off** their sales campaign last week and it is going very well.

- The boss wants to **kick off** the promotion with a full-page magazine ad.

- We have to wait for Mr. Mauvady. We can't **kick off** the meeting without the CEO!

- We will **kick off** the meeting at 10:00, so don't be late.

- What time will the talent show **kick off**?

60: look down on

Meaning
- To view disparagingly.

Usage
- A person can **look down on** another person's behavior or status.

Not Separable
- look down on

Examples
- The new CEO **looks down on** everyone on the management team that doesn't have an MBA.

- I thought my new coworkers would **look down on** me because I am a beginner at golf, but everyone is very nice and helpful.

- Discrimination happens when people **look down on** others who are different from them.

- Jack lives in a very wealthy area and **looks down on** anyone who lives in the poorer part of town.

- You shouldn't **look down on** someone or treat them badly.

- The rich couple **looks down on** their new son-in-law because he comes from a working class family.

Quiz 6

Fill in the blank space with the correct answer choice:

1. Jack _____ telling his wife that he was laid off.
    a. held back
    b. held on
    c. held on to
    d. hung out

2. Joe is _____ his belief that the company will not go bankrupt.
    a. giving away
    b. going over
    c. holding on to
    d. holding back

3. I had to _____ for a long time so I hung up the phone.
    a. hold back
    b. hold on to
    c. hold on
    d. hang around

4. I didn't get hurt in the accident because I was _____.
    a. hanging out
    b. hanging on
    c. giving in
    d. giving up

5. Teenagers like to _____ in Times Square at night.
    a. hang around
    b. hang on
    c. hold back
    d. hold on

6. Tom tried to _____ some girl at the bar and she punched him!
    a. hook up with
    b. keep on
    c. kick off
    d. look into

7. What time will the dinner party _____ ?
    a. kick back
    b. kick off
    c. look for
    d. look forward to

8. I like to _____ in the park on a sunny day.
   - a. kick off
   - b. keep on
   - c. kick back
   - d. look out for

9. Jane's mother _____ her boyfriend because he's not rich.
   - a. looks into
   - b. looks for
   - c. looks down on
   - d. looks forward to

10. If you _____ exercising, you'll continue loosing weight.
    - a. hook up
    - b. keep on
    - c. look like
    - d. kick back

Practice Section 6

Now, it's your turn to practice and use the phrasal verbs that you studied. Answer the following questions. Write a complete sentence using the given phrasal verb.

1. Where do you usually **hang out** on the weekend? Who do you **hang around** with?

2. Do you **hang on to** something when you ride the train?

3. Have you ever **held back** from doing something?

4. Have you had to **hold on** the phone recently?

5. What memories do you **hold on to**?

6. Have you **hooked up** with someone recently?

7. Are you trying to **keep on** doing something?

8. Where do you like to **kick back**?

9. Have you ever **kicked off** a meeting or a game?

10. What do you think of someone who **looks down on** another person?

Confusing Words 6: Fun and Funny

Fun

We use **fun** to say that something is enjoyable. There are four ways you can use **fun**:
- Something is **fun**: Going up the Sky Tree was fun.
- You have **fun** somewhere: I always have fun in NYC.
- You have **fun** doing something: Jane has fun playing tennis with her friends.
- You have **fun** with someone: Jack is having fun with his friends tonight.

Be careful! We do not say: "I was **fun**" If something is **fun**, and you want to talk about your experience, you can say: "It was **fun**."

> A: How was the amusement park?
> B: Oh, It was **fun**. *Not, I was fun.*

Funny

We use **funny** to say that something makes us laugh. That is the difference between **fun** and **funny**. **Fun** means enjoyable or enjoyment. Something or someone that is **funny** makes you laugh:

- My friend Ed is **funny**. He tells great jokes.
- That comedian was **funny**!
- When you see someone laughing, but you are not sure why he or she is laughing, you can ask them, "What's so **funny**?"

Funny is also used to mean strange or odd when we use "sense" verbs (smell, taste, look, feel, sound, seem). Something smells, tastes, looks, feels, sounds, or seems **funny**
- This milk smells **funny**. Maybe it is outdated.
- Does this hairstyle look **funny** to you?
- The engine sounds **funny** I think we need to have the car serviced.

61: look for

Meaning
- To search.

Usage
- A person or group of people can **look for** something or someone.

Not Separable
- **look for**

Examples
- The boss asked Jack to **look for** potential clients in New York and Atlanta.

- I was **looking for** my red pen, but I couldn't find it. I think someone took it from my desk.

- Jane **looked for** Bob's email address, but it wasn't in the database.

- I heard that Cathy is **looking for** a new boyfriend. Why don't you ask her for a date?

- The police are **looking for** the bank robber.

- I was **looking for** information about my ancestors online.

62: look forward to

Meaning
- To anticipate with a feeling of pleasure and excitement.

Usage
- A person can **look forward to** something or doing something. **Look forward to** is used to show that you are anticipating an upcoming event with pleasure and excitement. You can also use **look forward to** in a negative sentence to show displeasure toward an upcoming event. **Look forward to** is followed by a noun or gerund.

Not Separable
- **look forward to**

Examples
- We are all **looking forward to** the party on Friday.

- The boss is **looking forward to** seeing our quarterly sales report. I hope we won't disappoint him.

- I'm **looking forward to** seeing my sister next week in New York.

- I'm **looking forward to** the concert. I love that group.

- Ugh! I'm not **looking forward to** going to the dental office tomorrow.

- I'm not **looking forward to** Jack's party, but I have to go. His parties are always boring.

63: look into

Meaning
- To check or investigate something.

Usage
- A person or a group of people can **look into** something. You **look into** something in order to obtain more information about it.

Not Separable
- look into

Examples

- We are **looking into** the possibility of opening a branch office in Singapore.

- I asked the IT department to **look into** the problem we are having with the email server.

- I think we should **look into** remodeling the lobby of the office. It looks old and the furniture looks drab.

- Jane is **looking into** a restaurant where we can have our end of year party.

- The company always **looks into** the background of all potential employees.

- The bank balance is not correct. I need to **look into** it.

64: look like

Meaning
- To resemble someone or something physically.

Usage
- A person, animal, or thing can look like another. We can use modifiers such as **look** a little **like**, **look** a lot **like**, etc.

Not Separable
- **look like**

Examples
- I think the new sales manager **looks like** Tom Hanks. Don't you think so?

- Jack's girlfriend is tall, thin, and pretty. She **looks like** a fashion model.

- Who do you **look like** in your family?

- The new boss **looks** a little bit **like** a monkey.

- I think I **look like** my mother, and my sister looks like my father.

- That cloud **looks** a lot **like** an alligator.

65: look out for

Meaning
- To be diligently aware of something.

Usage
- A person can **look out for** something or someone.

Not Separable
- **look out for**

Examples
- Jack went to the trade show in Vegas, so I told him to **look out for** our customers there.

- **Look out for** that low tree branch in front of the house. You don't want to hit your head.

- I am **looking out for** Jane's car. She should be coming soon.

- We need to **look out for** anyone wearing a blue uniform. Those people are from the security company and they can help us.

- When you cross the street, **look out for** oncoming traffic.

- **Look out for** the postman. I am expecting a package today.

66: look over

Meaning
- To review something; to proofread for errors.

Usage
- A person or a group of people can **look over** something.

Separable
- **look over** something
- **look** something **over**

Examples
- All new employees should carefully **look over** their emails before sending them out.

- Please have the legal department **look over** the lease for the new building.

- Please **look over** the new employee handbook. If you have any questions, contact the HR department.

- I was **looking over** the schedule and found two conflicting appointments.

- Can you **look over** this report for me?

- Joe was **looking** his phone bill **over** and found some incorrect charges.

67: look up to

Meaning
- To admire someone.

Usage
- A person can **look up to** another person. You can **look up to** someone you know personally, or a well-known person.

Not Separable
- **look up to**

Examples
- Our CEO is a well-respected man both in the company and in the community. Many people **look up to** him as a source of inspiration.

- Joey **looks up to** his sports heroes and wants to become a pro baseball player when he grows up.

- Who do you **look up to** as a model CEO?

- Did you **look up to** your mom or dad when you were a child?

- Little Tommy **looks up to** his father very much.

- I always **looked up to** my parents when I was a kid.

68: luck out

Meaning
- To experience luck; to be fortunate.

Usage
- A person, animal, or business can **luck out**.

Not Separable
- **luck out**

Examples
- We **lucked out** when ABC company accepted our sales agreement.

- I **lucked out**. My new boss is really great!

- Jack **lucked out** when he got free tickets to the Yankee game.

- Did you **luck out** at the casino in Las Vegas?

- Lori **lucked out** and won the lottery!

- Apple really **lucked out** when it released the iPod.

69: make up (with)

Meaning
- To reconcile.

Usage
- People can **make up** after a disagreement. We generally use **make up** to talk about individuals (like couples, friends, neighbors, etc.) reconciling. **Make up** is not used when referring to businesses or governments. We use **make up with** when a direct object is used.

Not Separable
- **make up**
- **make up** with [someone]

Examples
- Have you **made up** with your girlfriend yet?

- I think there is no possibility that Jack and his wife will **make up**.

- **Making up** is more difficult than breaking up.

- We **made up**, kissed, and everything is fine now.

- I'm glad Steve **made up** with his wife. They are such a nice couple.

- After two weeks of arguing the couple finally **made up**.

70: mix up

Meaning
- To confuse.

Usage
- A person or something can mix up a situation or a thing.

Separable
- **mix up** something
- **mix** something **up**

Examples
- If you **mix up** the customer's files, the sales team will be very upset.

- I **mixed up** the time of today's meeting with tomorrow's meeting time.

- Don't **mix** the wires **up**. If you do, you may break the equipment.

- I **mixed up** the exits in the train station and was lost for thirty minutes.

- A good actor never **mixes** their lines **up**.

- The bank **mixed up** my first and last names on my account.

Quiz 7

Fill in the blank space with the correct answer choice:

1. I was _____ a gift for my boss at the shop on Madison Ave.
    a. looking like
    b. looking forward to
    c. looking down on
    d. looking for

2. Please _____ the FedEx guy. I need some shipping labels.
    a. look into
    b. look out for
    c. look forward to
    d. look like

3. I need to _____ why my name is misspelled on my paycheck.
    a. look down on
    b. look like
    c. look into
    d. look up to

4. Don't you think that woman _____ Julia Roberts?
    a. looks like
    b. looks out for
    c. looks over
    d. looks into

5. I'm _____ seeing my grandparents when I go home for Christmas.
    a. looking like
    b. looking for
    c. looking forward to
    d. looking down on

6. You always need to _____ the check at a restaurant.
    a. look up to
    b. luck out
    c. look over
    d. look out for

7. Jack _____ when he met Hiroko. She's smart, funny, and beautiful.
    a. looked over
    b. lucked out
    c. made up
    d. mixed up

8. They _____ and even decided to get married!
   a. mixed up
   b. made up
   c. picked out
   d. picked up

9. Michael always _____ his uncle Tony. He was a great man.
   a. looked up to
   b. looked over
   c. put away
   d. put down

10. I _____ my appointments and visited the wrong customer on the wrong day.
   a. looked up to
   b. picked out
   c. put away
   d. mixed up

Practice Section 7

Now, it's your turn to practice and use the phrasal verbs that you studied. Answer the following questions. Write a complete sentence using the given phrasal verb.

1. Have you **looked for** something recently?

2. What are you **looking forward to**?

3. Have you **looked into** something recently?

4. Who do you **look like**?

5. Do you need to **look out for** someone or something?

6. What have you **looked over** recently?

7. Who did you **look up to** when you were young?

8. Do you know someone who **lucked out** recently?

9. Do you know two people who have recently **made up**?

10. Have you **mixed up** something recently?

Confusing Words 7 Hard vs. Hardly

Hard

Hard is used as an adjective and has the opposite meaning of "soft".
- A bagel has a hard crust and a soft inside.
- Steel is harder than wood.

In addition, **hard** is used to mean "difficult."
- The final exam was harder than I expected.
- Some people find it hard to use the subway in Tokyo.

Hard is also used as an adverb and means, "using a lot of effort or with a lot of energy." **Hard** generally comes after the verb.
- He said he studied very **hard** to pass the exam.
- We worked **hard** on the report and finally finished it on time.

Hardly

Hardly is also an adverb but means "scarcely" or "barely." **Hardly** generally comes before the verb.
- It **hardly** rained this summer, so the water supply is low.
- The trains **hardly** come between midnight and 6:00am.

Thus, in a way, the adverb **hardly** can have the opposite meaning of the adverb **hard**. Compare these two sentences:

- Jack worked **hard** on the project all day. *Jack used a lot of effort.*
- Jack **hardly** worked on the project all day. *Jack used very little effort.*

71: mull over

Meaning
- To think about or consider something carefully.

Usage
- A person can **mull over** an important decision or plan, etc.

Separable
- **mull over** something
- **mull** something **over**

Examples
- The boss is **mulling over** expanding the business in Asia.

- I think you have an interesting idea. Let me **mull** it **over** for a few days and I'll let you know my decision.

- I'm **mulling over** where to go on my next vacation.

- Our customer is still **mulling** our proposal **over**. I hope we get a reply soon.

- Can you give me your decision now, or do you need more time to **mull** it **over**?

- So here is my proposal. Please **mull** it **over**, and tell me you opinion at the next meeting.

72: pick out

Meaning
- To choose; to select

Usage
- A person can **pick out** something. Generally we use **pick out** to talk about a person's action not a company's action.

Separable
- **pick out** something
- **pick** something **out**

Examples
- The boss said I should go to the cell phone shop and **pick out** a smartphone.

- I **picked out** some nice flowers to put at the reception desk.

- Jack said he **picked out** two nice books on marketing for Joe's birthday present.

- Did you **pick out** a birthday card for Jane?

- I **picked out** a nice tie to wear with my blue suit.

- I have to go to the bakery and **pick** a cake out **for** Gloria's birthday.

73: pick up

Meaning
- (1) To retrieve. (2) To buy.

Usage
- (1) A person can **pick up** an object or another person.
- (2) A person can **pick up** goods.

Separable
- **pick up** something
- **pick** something **up**

Examples
- (1) What time should we **pick up** the boss at JFK Airport?

- (1) Can you **pick** me **up** at the bus stop?

- (1) Please help me **pick up** the trash from the floor.

- (2) I am going to **pick** a pizza **up** for dinner.

- (2) Let's **pick up** some donuts on the way to the meeting.

- (2) Tomorrow is the CEO's birthday. Let's **pick up** a cake.

74: pop up

Meaning
- To appear suddenly

Usage
- We use **pop up** in any situation when something suddenly happens or occurs. A person can **pop up** somewhere, a situation can **pop up**, and an idea can **pop up** in someone's mind.

Not Separable
- pop up

Examples
- I haven't seen Jack for a while. I wonder when he'll **pop up** again.

- I was surprised when Bob **popped up** at the meeting yesterday.

- Just one day after they fixed the server, a new problem **popped up** with it.

- A thunderstorm **popped up** when we were in Dallas and our flight was delayed for three hours.

- Great idea, Jim. Did that just **pop up** or had you thought about it before?

- A few new issues **popped up** during the meeting and we found a solution to all of them.

75: put away (1)

Meaning
- To replace or return to the original place.

Usage
- A person can **put away** something in it's original or usual storage place.

Separable
- **put away** something
- **put** something **away**

Examples
- After the meeting we need to **put away** all of these files and binders.

- I thought I **put away** the two-hole punch, but now I can't find it.

- The meeting will start now, so please **put away** your cell phones.

- We finished washing and **putting away** the dishes at 9:30pm.

- Please **put away** your toys when you finish with them.

- I'm going to **put** my sweaters **away** until next winter.

76: put away (2)

Meaning
- To consume, as in eat or drink.

Usage
- A person (or an animal) can **put away** a food or drink. **Put away** is used in casual English conversations to mean eat or drink.

Separable
- **put away** something
- **put** something **away**

Examples
- The boss **put away** a whole bottle of wine last night.

- I **put away** three donuts during the meeting. Now my stomach hurts.

- How many hot dogs can you **put away** at one time?

- I think I **put away** that drink too quickly. I feel drunk already!

- Greg **put** four cocktails **away** in a half hour!

- I love pizza so much I can easily **put away** four slices.

77: put down

Meaning
- To insult; to disparage

Usage
- A person can **put down** another person.

Separable
- **put down** someone
- **put** someone **down**

Examples
- The CEO **put down** all of the managers at the meeting because none of them achieved the target.

- When his peers **put** him **down**, Jack became more determined to succeed.

- I'm not trying to **put** you **down**, I just think your idea for improving sales needs more work.

- I don't like Bob. He always **puts** me **down**.

- Don't put me **down**. I am trying as hard as I can to hit the ball.

- The bully tried to **put** me **down**, but I refused to let him bother me.

78: put off

Meaning
- To postpone.

Usage
- A person can **put off** something for a later time. We **put off** events, appointments, etc.

Separable
- **put off** something
- **put** something **off**

Examples
- The boss wants us to **put** the meeting **off** until tomorrow afternoon.

- Don't **put off** writing the report until the last minute.

- Jack **put off** going to the store until the afternoon, and all of the iPhones were sold out by the time he got there.

- We should **put off** opening a branch office in Mexico City until next year.

- We **put off** the golf game until next week.

- I heard Jenny **put** her wedding **off** because her mom needed an operation.

79: put on

Meaning
- To dress

Usage
- A person can **put on** their clothes. You can also **put** clothes **on** another person. **Put on** is the action of dressing.

Separable
- **put on** something
- **put** something **on**

Examples
- Even in the summer, I **put on** a suit every morning.

- The boss told us to **put on** jackets when the CEO arrives in the office.

- I **put on** my favorite shirt this morning and accidentally spilled coffee on it!

- Jane **put on** two different colored socks today. She looks strange.

- Katie **put** a teddy-bear outfit **on** her baby. How cute!

- I **put** my pajamas **on** and relaxed in front of the fireplace.

---

*Note: **Put on** is an action:
- I put on my hat

Wear is a state:
- I wear my hat all winter long.

80: put out (1)

Meaning
- To extinguish.

Usage
- A person can **put out** a fire, a cigarette, or some other burning object.

Separable
- **put out** something
- **put** something **out**

Examples
- This tool is used to **put out** the flame of a candle.

- The CEO started smoking in the meeting room, and the hotel manager asked him to **put** it **out**.

- If you do not carefully **put out** your campfire, it may continue burning for a long time.

- Why are you **putting** your cigarette **out** on the carpet? Are you drunk?

- Please **put out** that cigar. There is no smoking here.

- The fire department **put** the fire **out** in less than one hour.

Quiz 8

Fill in the blank space with the correct answer choice:

1. Thanks for the presentation and the information. We need some time to _____ before making a decision.
    - a. use it up
    - b. clear it up
    - c. rule it out
    - d. mull it over

2. No matter what problems _____, Jack can handle them.
    - a. look over
    - b. pop up
    - c. pick out
    - d. put down

3. Every morning I _____ Tom at his house and drive him to the office.
    - a. pick out
    - b. make up
    - c. pick up
    - d. put away

4. I want to _____ something nice for my wife for her birthday. Do you have any suggestions?
    - a. luck out
    - b. make up
    - c. pick out
    - d. put down

5. My husband always helps me wash and _____ the dishes.
    - a. put down
    - b. put away
    - c. make up
    - d. mix up

6. Wow! We _____ so much beer last night.
    - a. looked over
    - b. put away
    - c. looked up to
    - d. looked like

7. The boss _____ Joe in front of the CEO. It was unbelievable.
    - a. put on
    - b. put out
    - c. put down
    - d. put off

8. The salesman was drunk, so he _____ his cigarette in his dessert plate.
   - a. put up with
   - b. put up
   - c. put together
   - d. put out

9. Tom never _____ doing what he needs to do. He's such an organized person.
   - a. puts off
   - b. puts on
   - c. puts up
   - d. puts up with

10. I _____ sweatpants and a T-shirt after I got home from work.
    - a. put together
    - b. put in
    - c. put on
    - d. put up with

Practice Section 8

Now, it's your turn to practice and use the phrasal verbs that you studied. Answer the following questions. Write a complete sentence using the given phrasal verb.

1. What have you **picked out** recently?

2. Have you **picked** someone **up** recently? Has someone **picked** you **up** recently?

3. When was the last time you had a good idea **pop up**?

4. Do usually you **put** your things **away** when you are finished using them?

5. How many slices of pizza can you **put away**?

6. Has someone tried to **put** you **down** recently?

7. Have you **put off** something recently?

8. What did you **put on** this morning?

9. Have you ever **put out** a fire?

Confusing Words 8 Hope and Wish

Wish

We generally use **wish** in imaginary or hypothetical situations:
- I **wish** I had a cat. ← *I don't have a cat, but I want one.*
- I **wish** Jane were here.
- I **wish** I were taller.

*Note: In regular, conversational English, most speakers use I **wish** I were or I **wish** someone were:
- I **wish** Jane were here.
- I **wish** I were a better dancer.

Hope

We generally use **hope** in real situations to indicate a desired outcome.
- I **hope** it doesn't rain today. ← *The forecast says rain, but I would be happier if it did not rain.*
- I **hope** the train comes on time.
- I **hope** the exam is cancelled.

81: put out (2)

Meaning
- To publish or make available for sale.

Usage
- A person or a business can **put out** something. We usually use **put out** to talk about a publication or product that is offered to the public.

Separable
- **put out** something
- **put** something **out**

Examples
- Our company **puts out** new brochures every year.

- Before we print and **put** this manual **out**, we had better send it to the HR department once more for their final approval.

- That beer company **puts out** a different seasonal beer every three months.

- I can't wait for my favorite pop star to **put out** her new song!

- That company **put out** a new catalog last week.

- I heard Sony will **put** a new tablet **out** next month.

82: put together

Meaning
- To assemble; to construct; to organize (an event)

Usage
- A person or a business can **put together** something. **Put together** can be used to mean construct something, or organize some event.

Separable
- **put together** something
- **put** something **together**

Examples
- We hired a company to **put together** the new conference room furniture.

- Our CEO decided to **put** a golf tournament **together** with our best customers.

- Can you please **put together** a report containing sales figures for the past three years?

- Jane **put together** a nice dinner party for us last night.

- I **put** the furniture from IKEA **together** in the afternoon.

- The bank **put together** a special package for new customers.

83: put up

Meaning
- To hang or display something.

Usage
- A person or a business can **put up** something. The thing we **put up** is generally for information (like a sign) or decoration (like art).

Separable
- **put up** something
- **put** something **up**

Examples
- The meeting room looks much nicer since we **put up** that picture of the New York City skyline.

- We are not allowed to **put up** any pictures or posters on the walls in this apartment.

- I **put up** a sign in the window to attract more customers.

- Let's **put** this painting **up** in the living room. It will look nice there.

- The new coffee shop **put up** fliers all over town.

- I'm going to **put** this poster **up** on the wall in my office.

84: put up with

Meaning
- To tolerate.

Usage
- A person can or cannot **put up with** something or someone. In general, we usually use **put up with** in a negative sentence.

Not Separable
- **put up with**

Examples
- Jane is always gossiping about the other coworkers. I can't **put up with** her anymore.

- I can't **put up with** the smell coming from Bob's office. Somebody needs to tell him he should use deodorant.

- It's so hot in the office today. I can't **put up with** it.

- He smokes and he drinks a lot. How can you **put up with** him?

- I can't **put up with** the noise from my neighbor's apartment any more.

- Joe is a lazy guy. How can **you put up** with him?

85: ramp up

Meaning
- To increase or cause an increase.

Usage
- A person or a business can **ramp up** profit, sales, effort, etc.

Separable
- **ramp up** something
- **ramp** something **up**

Examples
- This past quarter, we **ramped up** profits by 13%.

- We'll need to **ramp up** production in order to meet demand for our new product.

- After the fire in the warehouse, the company **ramped up** the number of safety procedures.

- Security in the airport was **ramped up** when the president arrived.

- Because of the rise in transportation cost, the supermarkets have **ramped** prices **up**.

- After **ramping up** our marketing efforts, we had an increase in sales.

86: rule out

Meaning
- To prevent something from happening.

Usage
- A person or a circumstance can **rule out** something

Separable
- **rule out** something
- **rule** something **out**

Examples
- The heavy rain yesterday afternoon **ruled out** our golf game.

- The boss didn't approve our plan, but he didn't **rule** it **out** either. We need to wait for his final decision.

- Forgetting to punch in at the factory **ruled out** Mike's chance of getting a salary raise.

- The drop in sales **ruled out** the company's ability to give everyone a summer bonus.

- We only have an hour of free time. That **rules out** going to see a movie today.

- Our competitor has opened two branches in New York. That **rules out** our chances of expanding there.

87: run away (from)

Meaning
- To escape; to break free; to avoid.

Usage
- A person or an animal **can run** away from somewhere. **Run away** can also be used to mean to avoid doing something one is responsible to do. We use **run away from** when a direct object is used.

Not Separable
- **run away (from)**

Examples
- Jane! Why did you **run away from** me last night. Don't you love me?

- Tommy **ran away from** home when he was 13 and joined the circus.

- I put a fence around my house to keep my dogs from **running away**.

- The prison has a very advanced security system. It's impossible for anyone to **run away**.

- My dog tried to **run away from** me, but I caught her.

- The bank robber **ran away**, but was caught later in the day.

88: run into (1)

Meaning
- To meet by chance.

Usage
- A person can **run into** another person.

Not Separable
- **run into**

Examples
- Jack said he **ran into** Jon Bon Jovi in the hotel lobby.

- I hope I don't **run into** my ex-girlfriend at the club tonight.

- If you **run into** Jane at the party, tell her I said hello!

- We **ran into** several customers at the trade show in Vegas last week.

- I **ran into** an old friend from high school last night.

- Who did you **run into** at your family reunion?

89: run into (2)

Meaning
- To collide.

Usage
- A person or an object can **run into** a person or object.

Not Separable
- **run into**

Examples
- Bob was rushing to leave the office and **ran into** his secretary. She dropped all of her files and a cup of coffee.

- If you drive too closely to the car in front of you, you might **run into** it.

- The truck's brakes malfunctioned and it **ran into** a parked car.

- Jack was texting while driving and **ran into** a garbage truck.

- I **ran into** the lamppost with my car and damaged the bumper.

- Don't ride your bicycle here. You may **run into** someone.

90: run out of

Meaning
- To use or exhaust the supply of; to consume all of something

Usage
- A person or a business can **run out of** something. That something can be tangible goods such as food or office supplies, or intangible things such as time or air.

Not Separable
- **run out of**

Examples
- If you **run out of** supplies like pens or folders, just ask the office manager.

- We **ran out of** toner for the copy machine, and they can't deliver it until tomorrow, so we can't make any copies.

- Tom never seems to **run out of** excuses for being late.

- If we do not hurry we will **run out of** time. The report is due by the end of the day.

- I **ran out of** milk, so I need to go to the store.

- The ice cream shop **ran out of** chocolate ice cream!

Quiz 9

Fill in the blank space with the correct answer choice:

1. His company will finally _____ a new model this year.
   - a. put out
   - b. put in
   - c. put down
   - d. put up with

2. The boss doesn't like the picture Jack _____ in the office.
   - a. put in
   - b. put up
   - c. put together
   - d. put down

3. Jane couldn't _____ her husband's behavior any more.
   - a. put down
   - b. put off
   - c. put up with
   - d. put together

4. I _____ Jack at the coffee shop yesterday.
   - a. ran away
   - b. put on
   - c. ran into
   - d. put up

5. We _____ a nice presentation, but the boss rejected our idea.
   - a. put up with
   - b. put down
   - c. put together
   - d. put on

6. If you try to _____, you will surely get caught.
   - a. put up
   - b. run away
   - c. put out
   - d. put down

7. Joe lost his balance on the bike and _____ a fence.
   - a. ran out of
   - b. took back
   - c. ran into
   - d. showed up

133

8. What is the best way to _____ output in the factory?
   a. put together
   b. put up
   c. ramp up
   d. rule out

9. We need a Plan B. The boss _____ our marketing proposal.
   a. ruled out
   b. put up
   c. put together
   d. ramped up

10. The HR department _____ employee manuals. They need to have more printed.
    a. ran out of
    b. ran over
    c. ran away
    d. ran into

Practice Section 9

Now, it's your turn to practice and use the phrasal verbs that you studied. Answer the following questions. Write a complete sentence using the given phrasal verb.

1. What did your favorite company **put out** this year?

2. Have you **put** something **together** recently?

3. If someone gave you a painting, where would you **put** it **up**?

4. Is there someone or something you can't **put up with**?

5. Does your company need to **ramp up** sales?

6. Did your partner, spouse, or boss recently **rule out** one of your ideas?

7. Have you ever had a pet that **ran away**?

8. Have you **run into** someone recently?

9. Have you ever **run into** something and hurt yourself?

10. Have you **run out of** something recently?

Confusing Words 9 Meet Vs. See

Meet

We use **meet** when we talk about the first time we spend time with someone. So the first time you ever stand face-to-face with someone you usually say, "It's nice to **meet** you." We only use "It's nice to **meet** you," the first time we **meet** someone. Here are some other examples of using **meet** this way:

- I am going to **meet** my sister's new boyfriend tomorrow night.
- David **met** his wife at a party.
- I **met** John about ten years ago.

We also use **meet** when we make an appointment or plans, or have a schedule.

- I suggested we **meet** on Friday.
- Let's **meet** tomorrow at 10:00 at the coffee shop.
- Joe and Tom are **meeting** at the library after school to study.

See

We use **see** when we talk about spending time with someone when it is not the first time. It could be a planned event or an unexpected situation. So, when you make plans with someone you have met before, you can say: "I am looking forward to **seeing** you."

- I am supposed to **see** Tomoko after school tomorrow.
- Jenny is coming back to Osaka from Spain. I can't wait to **see** her.
- It's nice to **see** you again!

91: run over (1)

Meaning
- To review; to look over; to analyze.

Usage
- A person can **run over** something. When you **run over** something you review it for errors or problems.

Not Separable
- **run over**

Examples
- We need to **run over** the price list once more before having it printed.

- I need someone to help me **run over** this report.

- Let's **run over** the plan one more time to make sure we know what to do.

- Jack **ran over** the meeting minutes with the boss and they said everything looks ok.

- I **ran over** the meeting schedule with Jack today.

- The boss wants to **run over** the itinerary for the trade show.

92: run over (2)

Meaning
- To use more time than was allotted.

Usage
- An event (meeting, ceremony, speech, etc.) can **run over**.

Not Separable
- **run over**

Examples
- The CEO's speech **ran over**, so we need to extend the meeting a few more minutes.

- If the meeting **runs over** more than 10 minutes, the hotel will charge us an overtime fee.

- The concert **ran over** because the band did three encores.

- Sorry I'm late. The party **ran over**.

- Let me know if you think your presentation will **run over**.

- I think if we only schedule two hours for the party we will surely **run over**.

93: show up

Meaning
- To arrive.

Usage
- A person or a vehicle (bus, train, etc.) can **show up**.

Not Separable
- **show up**

Examples
- What time did Jane **show up** this morning?
- Why do you always **show up** to work late?
- The boss always **shows up** thirty minutes early.
- Dressing professionally and **showing up** on time are very important in this company.
- The bus **showed up** twenty minutes late.
- Jack **shows up** on time for class every day.

94: sleep in

Meaning
- To intentionally wake up later than usual.

Usage
- A person can sleep in when they wish to have more sleep.

Not Separable
- **sleep in**

Examples
- I can't **sleep in** on the weekend because my dog always wakes me up early.

- Let's **sleep in** tomorrow and then have brunch in SOHO.

- Please don't wake me up tomorrow. I want to **sleep in**.

- I think I'll **sleep in** until noon tomorrow. I'm so tired!

- I feel like **sleeping in** today. It's Sunday.

- Do you usually **sleep in** on the weekend?

Sleep in vs. **oversleep**:
When you sleep in, it's your plan ☺
- I love to sleep in on my day off.

When you oversleep, it's an accident!
- I overslept and missed my flight!

95: sort out

Meaning
- To find the solution to a problem.

Usage
- A person can **sort out** a problem, an issue, etc.

Separable
- **sort out** something
- **sort** something **out**

Examples
- We need to **sort out** how to sell more gizmos online.

- Have you **sorted out** the problems in the accounting report?

- I need to **sort out** a few more issues with this software before the go-live day.

- We **sorted** the issue **out** during our morning meeting, and the boss was satisfied with that.

- Our customer asked us to **sort** the problem **out** with the missed delivery.

- Can you please help me **sort out** who we can send to the trade show?

96: stick to

Meaning
- To continue doing something as planned or arranged

Usage
- A person can **stick to** a schedule, a plan, policy, a promise, etc.

Not separable
- **stick to** [something]

Examples
- We only have an hour for this meeting so we must **stick to** the agenda and not discuss other matters.

- We had good results, so I think we should **stick to** this marketing plan next quarter too.

- The boss **stuck to** his promise and gave everyone a half-day off on Friday.

- Let's **stick to** the original plan and buy mom a watch for her birthday.

- Even if the GPS tells me to turn right, I am going to **stick to** the current route.

- Bob! Please **stick to** the topic. This is an important meeting.

97: take after

Meaning
- To have a similar personality.

Usage
- A person can take after a parent or other relative.

Not Separable
- **take after** [someone]

Examples
- The new manager **takes after** his father, the CEO; both are stubborn and strict.

- Who do you **take after**, your mom or dad?

- My son surely **takes after** his mother.

- Jack **takes after** his dad. He's kind, outgoing, and helpful.

- I **take after** my mother, and Lori **takes after** my father.

- Little Tommy **takes after** his grandfather.

98: take apart

Meaning
- To disassemble.

Usage
- A person can **take** something **apart**.

Separable
- **take apart** something
- **take** something **apart**

Examples
- In order to move this desk into the elevator, we'll need to **take** it **apart**.

- Tommy **took apart** his dad's computer and upgraded the motherboard.

- In order to clean the coffee pot well, you should **take** it **apart**.

- Jane **took** her bracelet **apart** and now she can't put it back together.

- I **took apart** my computer this morning.

- Jack **took** his car **apart** and rebuilt it.

99: take back (1)

Meaning
- To return something to the place of purchase.

Usage
- A person can **take back** something that was purchased to the store.

Separable
- **take back** something
- **take** something **back**

Examples
- The company policy is no returns or refunds. Once you buy something, you can't **take** it **back**.

- Jane tried to **take back** the dress after she wore it to the wedding, but the shop refused.

- Can I **take** this **back** if it doesn't fit?

- I **took back** the bag I bought and exchanged it for a bigger one.

- I **took back** my shirt and got a refund.

- This item is final sale, so you can't **take** it **back**.

100: take back (2)

Meaning
- To retract or recant something that was said.

Usage
- A person can take back their statement.

Separable
- **take back** something
- **take** something **back**

Examples
- Let me **take** that **back**. I don't mean that sales are slow. I mean sales are not growing as quickly as we estimated.

- We need to **take back** our offer. The price we quoted is too low for us to make a good profit.

- I'm not going to **take back** what I said. You are a terrible boss, and I quit!

- If you do not **take back** what you said, I am going to leave you.

- You should **take back** what you said to her. She is very upset.

- You shouldn't talk to your mother like that. **Take** it **back**.

Quiz 10

Fill in the blank space with the correct answer choice:

1. I think we need to _____ the schedule once more before the meeting.
    a. run into
    b. run away
    c. run over
    d. run out of

2. Joe is handy and good at fixing things. He _____ his father.
    a. takes back
    b. takes after
    c. runs over
    d. runs into

3. His presentations are always boring and _____ .
    a. run into
    b. run over
    c. run out of
    d. run away

4. When Joe didn't _____ what he said, his wife walked out of the house.
    a. run over
    b. take apart
    c. take back
    d. run away

5. Bob _____ the server but he couldn't fix it.
    a. took after
    b. ran into
    c. took apart
    d. ran away

6. You can't _____ anything you buy at a sample sale.
    a. take back
    b. show up
    c. run over
    d. take apart

7. Why can't you _____ on time for the meeting!
    a. sleep in
    b. run over
    c. show up
    d. take back

147

8. Ah, tomorrow is Sunday. I can finally _____ !
   a. show up
   b. sleep in
   c. run away
   d. run over

9. Let's try to _____ the two problems on the last page of the contract.
   a. take back
   b. show up
   c. sort out
   d. stick to

10. Why can't you guys _____ the topic? We need to focus, please!
    a. sort out
    b. stick to
    c. take after
    d. run over

Practice Section 10

Now, it's your turn to practice and use the phrasal verbs that you studied. Answer the following questions. Write a complete sentence using the given phrasal verb.

1. Have you ever been to an event which **ran over**?

2. Have you **run over** anything with anyone recently?

3. Do you **show up** for work or school on time?

4. Do you like to **sleep in**? Did you sleep in today?

5. Did you need to **sort** anything **out** this week?

6. When you make a decision, do you usually **stick to** it?

7. Who do you **take after**?

8. Have you **taken** something **apart** recently?

9. Have you tried to **take** something **back** to a store recently?

10. Do you need to **take back** something you said recently?

Confusing Words 10 By Vs. Until

By

We use **by** to show that something finishes at a certain time or deadline. When you finish something **by** a certain time, day, date, etc., you complete the action when the deadline comes.

We use **by** with verbs that show completion or ending. For example, stop **by**, end **by**, finish **by**, complete **by**, arrive by, leave **by**, go **by**, come **by**, etc.

- If we arrive at the station **by** 3pm, we can catch the train.
- Please complete your essay **by** Friday.
- Can you finish work **by** 6 tonight? If so, we can catch a movie.

Until

We use **until** to show that something continues to a certain time or deadline. When you continue to do something **until** a certain time, day, date, etc, it means you continue doing that thing and when the certain time, day, date, etc. comes, you stop doing it.

We use **until** with verbs that show action or continuous movement. For example, stay **until**, have **until**, work **until**, study **until**, play **until**, drink **until**, eat **until**, etc.

- We have **until** 3pm to arrive at the station in order to catch the train.
- Jack will stay in New York **until** July.
- I'm working **until** 6 tonight.

101: take off (1)

Meaning
- To undress.

Usage
- A person can **take off** clothes, accessories such as eyeglasses or jewelry, or makeup.

Separable
- **take off** something
- **take** something **off**

Examples
- Can I **take off** my jacket and tie? It's really warm in the office.

- We are not supposed to **take off** our jackets and sit down until the CEO finishes his kick off speech.

- The boss's hairpiece fell off when he **took off** his hat.

- You look warm. Why don't you **take off** that sweater?

- Please **take off** your shoes when you enter the house.

- I **took** my jacket **off** and hung it up on the hook.

102: take off (2)

Meaning
- To leave the ground and begin flight.

Usage
- A bird, an airplane, or a flight can **take off**.

Not Separable
- **take off**

Examples
- The flight **took off** on time today.

- I like to go to the airport and watch the planes **take off**.

- The plane couldn't **take off** due to mechanical trouble.

- The flight will **take off** on schedule. Please fasten your seatbelts.

- What time does your flight **take off** tomorrow?

- The whole flock of birds **took off** together.

103: take out (of)

Meaning
- To extract; to remove.

Usage
- A person can **take out** something from it original or usual place. You can use **take out of** when you mention the place that the item came from.

Separable
- **take out** something
- **take** something **out**

Examples
- Can you **take out** the last paragraph of this report? I think it is unnecessary.

- The boss wants us to **take** two slides **out** of the presentation because it is too long.

- I want to **take out** the hard drive from my laptop but I'm not sure how to do it.

- **Take out** the ice and the scotch. I've had a tough day at the office.

- The dentist **took out** my wisdom tooth.

- I took a **pizza out** of the freezer for dinner.

104: tell off

Meaning
- To sharply criticize; to reprimand

Usage
- A person can **tell off** another person.

Separable
- **tell off** someone
- **tell** someone **off**

Examples
- The boss often **tells off** his staff, but rarely praises them.

- He **told** me **off** and then walked out of the room.

- Jane said she is going to **tell off** her husband as soon as he gets home.

- Don't talk to me like that. You can **tell off** your friends, but not your mother!

- The boss **told off** the receptionist for not giving him an important message.

- Joe's wife **told** him **off** when he came home late for dinner.

105: think over

Meaning
- To consider over a short period of time.

Usage
- A person can **think over** something. You **think** something **over** when you need some time to consider it carefully.

Separable
- **think over** something
- **think** something **over**

Examples
- The boss said he would **think over** our suggestion. At least he didn't say no.

- Jack said he needs time to **think over** what we discussed in the meeting.

- If you give the customer too much time to **think over** their purchase, you may lose the sale.

- I've **thought** it over carefully, and I've decided to marry her.

- Thanks for giving me the suggestion. Let me **think** it **over**.

- I need some time to **think over** what you said.

106: think up

Meaning
- To envision; to create in the mind.

Usage
- A person can **think up** a plan, an idea, an activity, etc.

Separable
- **think up** something
- **think** something **up**

Examples
- The sales manager **thought up** a great idea for selling more products.

- We need to **think up** a way to increase profits.

- Management said that couldn't **think up** a way to prevent the lay off.

- I can't **think up** anything now. I'll have to get back to you tomorrow.

- I **thought up** this book while I was having a lesson.

- I love pizza. I wonder who the first person was to **think** it **up**.

107: throw away

Meaning
- To discard; to dispose of.

Usage
- A person can **throw away** something.

Separable
- **throw away** something
- **throw** something **away**

Examples
- Jack said he accidentally **threw away** his wedding ring.

- In this city, we don't recycle paper. We just **throw** it **away**.

- Somebody **threw away** a perfectly good radio and Bob picked it up on the street.

- I don't have any of my toys from my childhood. I **threw** them **away**.

- I **threw away** my trash after lunch.

- Don't leave your trash here. Make sure you **throw** it **away** to the garbage can.

108: try on

Meaning
- To wear something in order to check the size, fit, look, etc.

Usage
- A person can **try on** clothes, shoes, eyeglasses, etc.

Separable
- **try on** something
- **try** something **on**

Examples
- I **tried on** the company uniform, but I don't like how it looks.

- This is such a nice shirt. I'm going to **try** it **on**.

- Excuse me. Is there somewhere I can **try on** these jeans?

- The sample sale had great prices, but there was no place to **try on** the clothes.

- I **tried on** three hats and then finally found one I like.

- The sneakers don't fit. I should have **tried** them **on** before I bought them.

109: turn away

Meaning
- To avert one's eyes, face, or body.

Usage
- A person can **turn away**. We use **turn away from** when a direct object is used.

Not Separable
- **turn away** (**from**) something / someone

Examples
- I had to **turn away** when the boss started discussing my poor performance.

- Please don't **turn away** when I am speaking to you. This is important.

- I **turned away** when I drove past the car accident.

- The movie star **turned away** from the paparazzi and got into the limousine.

- I **turned away** from the bright light.

- She **turned away** during the scary scene in the movie.

110: turn back

Meaning
- To reverse direction; to retreat; to return to the original place.

Usage
- A person or a vehicle can **turn back**. **Turn back** can also mean to cease moving forward on a project.

Not Separable
- **turn back**

Examples
- We are in the middle of negotiations now. There is no **turning back**.

- We got lost on the way to Jack's office, so we **turned back** and tried a different route.

- There is a restaurant over there. Let's **turn back** and go there.

- You can't **turn back** time.

- The hikers **turned back** when the storm approached.

- The road was closed so I **turned back** and took a another route.

Quiz 11

Fill in the blank space with the correct answer choice:

1. In the USA, people usually don't _____ their shoes when they enter a house.
    a. take back
    b. try on
    c. take out
    d. take off

2. On the Friday before a long weekend, everyone in my office usually _____ early.
    a. takes off
    b. tries on
    c. takes back
    d. thinks over

3. I _____ my laptop and started working right away.
    a. think over
    b. took out
    c. took off
    d. think up

4. I _____ so many pairs of shoes, but nothing matched my suit.
    a. took back
    b. tried on
    c. thought over
    d. turned away

5. I have to _____ what he said and then make a decision.
    a. take back
    b. take off
    c. think over
    d. tell off

6. We should _____ all of this old furniture when we move to the new house. It's not useable.
    a. take back
    b. take off
    c. think over
    d. throw away

7. Everyone in the office was surprised that Joe, who is the new guy, _____ such a great idea.
    a. took back
    b. took off
    c. told off
    d. thought up

8. She _____ while I was talking to her. How rude!
    a. took back   b. thought over
    c. tried on   d. turned away

9. If we don't _____ now, we might get caught in a storm. I hate driving in the rain.
    a. try on   b. take back
    c. turn back   d. take out

10. I can't believe Jack _____ the boss yesterday. He might get fired because of it.
    a. thought over   b. took back
    c. turned away   d. told off

Practice Section 11

Now, it's your turn to practice and use the phrasal verbs that you studied. Answer the following questions. Write a complete sentence using the given phrasal verb.

1. What was the first thing you **took off** when you got home yesterday?

2. Have you ever seen a plane **take off**?

3. Have you **taken** anything **out of** the freezer recently?

4. Has anyone told **you off** recently? Have you told someone off?

5. Have you **thought over** something recently?

6. Have you ever **thought up** a new dish or meal? What was it?

7. What did you **throw away** today?

8. What did you **try on** recently? Did you buy it?

9. What have you **turned away** from recently?

10. Have you needed to **turn back** because of weather or some other reason?

111: turn down (1)

Meaning
- To decrease volume or brightness.

Usage
- A person can turn down a TV, radio, light, music, etc..

Separable
- **turn down** something
- **turn** something **down**

Examples
- If you are going to watch YouTube videos in the office, please **turn down** the sound or use headphones.

- We **turned down** the lights, lit some candles and had a romantic dinner.

- The band at the wedding realized they were too loud and **turned down** the volume.

- Can you **turn down** the radio? I hate that song.

- Please **turn down** the TV. I am trying to study.

- I **turned** the light **down** and took a nap.

112: turn down (2)

Meaning
- To reject; to decline

Usage
- A person or a business can **turn down** a person, an invitation, an offer, etc.

Separable
- **turn down** something/someone
- **turn** something/someone **down**

Examples
- The boss **turned down** Jimmy for a promotion because of his bad attendance record.

- I offered to take Joe to the airport, but he **turned** me **down**.

- You cannot reapply for the position if you are **turned down** more than three times.

- Jane **turned down** Bob's invitation for a date. He's pretty heartbroken.

- The bank **turned down** my loan application.

- I asked her to marry me, but she **turned** me **down**.

113: turn off

Meaning
- To stop the electric current; to stop an electric item.

Usage
- A person can **turn off** a TV, radio, light, music, etc.

Separable
- **turn off** something
- **turn** something **off**

Examples
- I **turned off** all the lights before leaving the office.

- I never **turn off** my computer. Should I?

- Did you **turn off** the coffee maker?

- I **turned off** the alarm clock and went back to sleep.

- They **turned off** the air conditioner to save money.

- Can you please **turn off** the radio? I want to watch TV.

114: turn on

Meaning
- To start the electric current; to start an electric item.

Usage
- A person can **turn on** a TV, radio, light, music, etc.

Separable
- **turn on** something
- **turn** something **on**

Examples
- After you **turn on** the projector, it takes about one minute for the lamp to become bright.

- I **turn on** all of the lights when I study.

- Jack said he **turned on** the TV as soon as he heard the news.

- Do you like to **turn on** the TV during dinner?

- I **turn on** the TV every morning to check the weather.

- I always **turn** the radio **on** in the car.

115: turn out

Meaning
- To result; to end up; to become.

Usage
- A situation or a person can **turn out** in a certain way.

Not Separable
- **turn out**

Examples
- The party **turned out** well. Too bad you missed it.

- How did your meeting with the boss **turn out**?

- Did the contract negotiations **turn out** as expected?

- I heard you baked a cake. How did it **turn out**?

- The meeting **turned out** to be a success. Now, both labor and management are happy.

- Billy Joel dropped out of high school, but **turned out** to be a successful singer.

116: turn up (1)

Meaning
- To increase the volume or brightness.

Usage
- A person can **turn up** a TV, radio, light, music, etc.

Separable
- **turn up** something
- **turn** something **up**

Examples
- When I hear my favorite musician, I **turn up** the radio.

- You may damage your hearing if you **turn up** the volume too high while wearing headphones.

- I can't **turn up** this light any more. Maybe the light bulb is bad.

- I broke the speakers when I **turned** the volume **up** to 10.

- **Turn up** the TV. I can't hear it well.

- This is my favorite song. Please **turn** the radio **up**.

117: turn up (2)

Meaning
- To arrive.

Usage
- A person or a vehicle (bus, train, etc.) can **turn up**.

Not separable
- **turn up**

Examples
- The boss will be angry if you **turn up** late for the meeting.

- What time did the repairman **turn up** this morning?

- The trains in Tokyo usually **turn up** on time.

- She **turned up** at 6:00, which was three hours late.

- Jack **turned up** late for work and the boss was so angry.

- The busses in this town never **turn up** on time.

118: use up

Meaning
- To completely consume

Usage
- A person can **use up** something or **use** something **up**

Separable
- **use up** something
- **use** something **up**

Examples
- The CEO's speech **used up** half of the time that we scheduled for the meeting.

- I think online advertising is important, but I don't want to **use up** 50% of our budget on it.

- If you **use up** the paper in the copier, you can find more paper in the closet.

- Jack **used up** most of his marketing budget on travel.

- We won't be able to order more of that coffee until the summer, so try not to **use** it **up**.

- I **used up** all of the maple syrup we had when I made muffins last weekend.

119: wipe off

Meaning
- To clean the surface of something.

Usage
- A person can **wipe off** something.

Separable
- **wipe off** something
- **wipe** something **off**

Examples
- **Wipe off** that plate. It seems dirty.

- I tried to **wipe off** the stain on the counter but I couldn't do it.

- **Wipe off** your mouth. You have a milk moustache.

- We should **wipe** the glasses **off** before using them.

- Mom **wiped off** the spilled milk from the table.

- You should **wipe** that beach chair **off** before you sit down. It has a lot of sand on it.

120: work out

Meaning
- To exercise

Usage
- A person can **work out** with something or at a certain place.

Not Separable
- **work out**

Examples
- I wish I had time to **work out**. I'm so busy.

- Jack started **working out**. He looks good.

- Jane and her husband **work out** together.

- Ken **works out** at home with dumbbells.

- I was **working out** this morning and I feel good.

- Pat **works out** with weights at the gym.

Quiz 12

1. If you are never going to _____ on time, you will loose your credibility.
    - a. turn down
    - b. turn back
    - c. turn up
    - d. turn on

2. I heard Jane was _____ for the job.
    - a. turned down
    - b. turned out
    - c. turned up
    - d. turned back

3. Can you please _____ the light. Nobody is in the room.
    - a. turn up
    - b. turn out
    - c. turn on
    - d. turn off

4. It's time to _____ the music and the lights. Let's start the party!
    - a. turn in
    - b. turn up
    - c. turn back
    - d. turn out

5. The last time I _____ at a gym was when I was in college.
    - a. turned off
    - b. wiped off
    - c. worked out
    - d. turned down

6. Everything _____ exactly how we planned it.
    - a. turned down
    - b. turned off
    - c. turned up
    - d. turned out

7. Can you please _____ the dust from those bookshelves?
    - a. turn off
    - b. wipe off
    - c. work out
    - d. turn up

8. My husband is cheap and rarely _____ the air conditioner.
    a. turns back
    b. turns out
    c. turns on
    d. turns down

9. _____ that guitar. It's bothering the neighbors.
    a. Turn on
    b. Turn down
    c. Turn back
    d. Turn out

10. If we _____ the budget for this trade show, we won't be able to attend another one until next year.
    a. turn off
    b. wipe off
    c. use up
    d. turn up

Practice Section 12

Now, it's your turn to practice and use the phrasal verbs that you studied. Answer the following questions. Write a complete sentence using the given phrasal verb.

1. Do you **turn down** or **turn off** the lights when you go to sleep?

2. Has someone **turned** you **down** recently? Have you turned someone down recently?

3. Do you **turn off** your computer at night or just put it to sleep?

4. Have you cooked or tried to do something recently? How did it **turn out**?

5. Do you like to **turn on** the radio in the car?

6. Do you like to **turn up** the volume when you hear a good song?

7. Do you usually **turn up** on time or early for appointments?

8. Have you recently **used up** anything in your kitchen?

9. Do you **wipe off** the seats in a restaurant or station before sitting down?

10. Do you like to **work out**? How often do you work out?

Quiz Answer Key

	Q1	Q2	Q3	Q4	Q5	Q6
1	c	d	a	c	b	a
2	b	a	d	d	d	c
3	a	a	d	c	c	c
4	d	d	d	a	a	b
5	d	c	a	c	b	a
6	c	c	d	d	b	a
7	a	a	b	b	d	b
8	b	d	b	c	c	c
9	b	a	d	d	b	c
10	b	b	c	b	c	b

	Q7	Q8	Q9	Q10	Q11	Q12
1	d	d	a	c	d	d
2	b	b	b	b	a	a
3	c	c	c	b	b	d
4	a	c	c	c	b	b
5	c	b	c	c	c	c
6	c	b	b	a	d	d
7	b	c	c	c	d	b
8	b	d	c	b	d	c
9	a	a	a	c	c	b
10	d	c	a	b	d	c

Survival English Tip 1 – The Tip System in America

Introduction

Tipping is a big part of life in America. I have heard that **tipping** is quite a confusing idea to a lot of people because in many countries there is no **tipping** custom. Well, if you keep in mind the following ideas, you won't have any trouble leaving a **tip**.

Tipping Language

Tip is usually a noun, and a more formal word for **tip** is **gratuity**. We usually use **tip** in spoken English and **gratuity** in written English. We use the verbs leave and pay with **tip**. You can also use **tip** as a verb. Here are some examples:

Leave a tip
- I'm going to leave a nice **tip** for the waiter. He was great.
- Do you want me to leave the **tip**?

Pay a tip
- We don't need to pay a **tip** because it is included in the check.
- Jack is cheap. He never pays a big **tip**.

Tip as a verb
- I **tipped** the taxi driver five dollars.
- You don't need to **tip** a teacher or a store clerk.

Tipping Custom

We generally **tip** for services performed by waiters & waitresses, taxi drivers, hair stylists & barbers and delivery people. A 15% **tip** is average. A 20~25% **tip** would be mean good ~ great service. A 10% **tip** means you were dissatisfied.

We also **tip** about $1~2 per bag for a bellhop or doorman, $1~2 for a parking valet, and $2~3 per night for the housekeeper at a hotel.

In some restaurants, for groups bigger than four people, the **tip** may be added to the check by the restaurant. If so, it usually says "gratuity included," so please be sure to look over the check carefully before paying.

Survival English Tip 2 – Regular Greetings

Here is a sample conversation between two friends. I'm sure you have studied this before:

Brad: Hello. How are you?
Angela: I'm fine thank you, and you?
Brad: I'm fine thank you.

This is just a model conversation and there are many variations. It is important to know that a greeting in English always starts with a question, and there are two kinds of questions we use; how questions and what questions. Here are some examples of each:

How Questions:	What Questions:
How are you?	What's new?
How's it going?	What's up?
How's life?	What's going on?
How's everything?	What's shaking?

How

Let's study how questions first. Each of these how questions has the same meaning. How questions ask about our feeling or condition, so the answers are something like this:

How are you?	→ Not too bad
How's it going?	→ Pretty good
How's life?	→ Great!
How's everything?	→ I'm ok.

How questions, which are used as a greeting, are just greetings, so your response does not need to be very serious or deep. A simple response, like the examples above, is fine.

What

Each of these what questions has the same meaning. What questions ask about news or information about, so the answers are something like this:

What's new?	→ Not much, but I just ate lunch.
What's up?	→ It's a nice day today!
What's going on?	→ I'm going on vacation next week
What's shaking?	→ I heard the Yankees won last night!

What questions, which are used as a greeting, are also just greetings, and they are used to find a topic for small talk. Your answer can be about the weather, spots, or you can talk about something you did or will do.

When you greet your coworkers in the morning, the conversation will go something like this:

Jack: Hi Hiro.
Hiro: Hi Jack. How's it going?
Jack: Not too bad, and you?
Hiro: I'm going great. What's shaking?
Jack: Not much. I heard it's going to be hot today again.
Hiro: Yeah. Better drink lots of water!
Jack: Good idea. Catch you later.
Hiro: See you!

Survival English Tip 3 – Five Key Words To Order Food

The day you arrive in the US on vacation, a business trip, or for a new overseas post, you're going to be hungry. Quite possibly, your first meal may be at a fast food restaurant. Here are five essential words you'll want to remember to help you order food.

- Next!
- Meal (not 'set')
- Is that it?
- For here?
- To go?

When you walk into the shop, the clerk will greet you. They generally say, "**Next!**" with a loud, stern voice and no smile. Don't be alarmed. They are not angry with you. This is just their usual speaking style. The politeness level of speaking used by the staff in a casual, fast food restaurant or shop is much lower than what you would might expect in your country, so don't be surprised!

In the USA, we generally use phrases like Combo **Meal** (combo is short for combination) or Value **Meal**. So, a Big Mac Value **Meal** means you get a Big Mac, French Fries, and a drink.

The question, "**Is that it?**" is the usual way to say, "Would you like anything else?" It is often pronounced by the clerk quickly, like this: "**zad-IT?**" If you want to order something additional, now is your chance.

Once you have given your complete order, the clerk will ask, Is that for here or to go or the shorter form, **for here** or **to go**? For here means you will eat your food in the shop and they will put your food on a tray. To go means you will eat your food back in your hotel or home, and in this case, they will put your food in a bag.

By the way, the phrase **take out** is used when we talk about ordering food with someone, but we do not say **take out** to the clerk in a restaurant. For example:
Hiroko: Do you want to go to the Chinese restaurant?
Greg: I'm too tired to go. Let's just order **take out**.

Ok, so now, let's see these words in a sample conversation:

Clerk: **Next!**
Aki: Can I have a Big Mac Value **Meal**, please?
Clerk: What kind of drink?
Aki: Coke, please.
Clerk: **Is that it?**
Aki: Yes, that's it.
Clerk: **For here** or **to go?**
Aki: To go.

Happy Eating!

Survival English Tip 4 – American Culture

Knowing some aspects of American culture will make life in the USA more understandable and less stressful. I'm going to talk about the following four aspects of American culture; **individualism**, **time**, **productivity**, and **directness**.

Individualism

Individualism in American has its roots in the mid-nineteenth century when Americans moved with their families from the east coast to the west. Sponsored by a government program, you could take your family out west, settle on federal land, and that land would be yours to keep. This fueled America's individualistic spirit. Americans live by the idea that people are independent individuals who have the freedom and responsibility to live and manage their own lives. While Americans do value family and friends, their ultimate loyalty is to themselves. For example, you'll see your American coworkers taking their paid vacation time at the point in the year which is most convenient for them, not necessarily for the company. Whereas in Japan, group harmony is usually considered before individualism, Americans are less inclined to follow a group.

Time

There are a number of proverbs in English that relate to time. For example, "time is money," "time and tide wait for no man" and "there is no time like the present." Especially in business, Americans value time and for most Americans, doing things on time and being on time (especially for meetings) is important. On the other hand, in social situations, Americans tend to be slightly late. Nobody wants to be the first one at the party, so coming five or ten minutes late to a party is not uncommon.

Productivity

Americans value hard work and having a strong work ethic. Compared to those in many European countries, Americans tend to work more hours and receive less vacation time.

Americans believe that working hard produces results, and they have a sense of personal pride when goals are accomplished. Thus, Americans value productivity. Working hard all day and accomplishing your work by quitting time (often 5:30 or 6:00pm) is desirable. Americans tend to judge themselves and other people based on their productivity and achievements.

Directness

In general, Americans tend to speak directly and frankly. They value clear communication and are often outspoken about their opinions. An exception to this is when Americans need to give bad news or negative feedback. For example, when Person A expresses his opinion, and asks Person B about it, if person B disagrees, he might express his disagreement more indirectly using a phrase such as, "Well, that's a good idea but…"

Survival English Tip 5 – Doctors, hospitals, clinics

In the US, we generally have a family doctor, also known as a primary care doctor. We visit this doctor in his or her private office. Sometimes this office is called a clinic. A doctor's office is a place with just one doctor and his staff. A clinic is a large place with several doctors. A hospital is a large building with many doctors and beds. You can stay overnight in a hospital, but not at a clinic or doctor's office. The important difference is:

- You go to the doctor's office or a clinic when it is not an emergency, like a cold, a rash, or a check-up.
- You go to a hospital when is for an emergency (like a broken leg, severe wound, accident, etc.) or for an operation.

You can say go to the doctor or see the doctor.
- I went to the doctor yesterday for a check-up.
- I had a bad cold so I decided to see the doctor.

To go to the doctor's office or a clinic, you need an appointment. We usually make a doctor's appointment and see the doctor. Once we make an appointment, we have an appointment. Again, you can also say that you are going to see the doctor:
- I made a doctor's appointment for April 3rd.
- I have a doctor's appointment at 3:00 this afternoon.
- I want to see the doctor about that pain in my back.

When you have an emergency, you go to the emergency room in a hospital. To go to the emergency room, you do not need an appointment. The emergency room is the place in the hospital where people with serious medical emergencies go, or are brought by an ambulance.

- I went to the emergency room after I fell off the ladder.
- The ambulance took Jack to the emergency room.

If the doctor in the emergency room thinks your condition is serious, you may be admitted to the hospital. In that case, we would say you are in the hospital.

- I was admitted to the hospital for testing after the accident.
- Jack is in the hospital for an operation.

Congratulations! You've reached the end of the book and have probably discovered I've actually put 120 Phrasal Verbs here!
I hope you enjoyed my surprise.
Thanks again for studying with me ☺

Other paperbacks & eBooks by Michael DiGiacomo

Made in the USA
Monee, IL
07 May 2020